CAPACITY BUILDING FOR NGOs

CAPACITY BUILDING FOR NGOs
Making it Work

Rick James and John Hailey

INTRAC
International NGO Training and Research Centre

INTRAC, the International NGO Training and Research Centre, was set up in 1991 to provide specially designed training, consultancy and research services to organisations involved in international development and relief. Our goal is to improve NGO performance by exploring policy issues and by strengthening management and organisational effectiveness.

First published in 2007 in the UK by
INTRAC
PO Box 563
Oxford
OX2 6RZ
United Kingdom

Tel: +44 (0)1865 201851
Fax: +44 (0)1865 201852
Email: info@intrac.org
website: www.intrac.org

Reprinted in 2009

ISBN 978-1-905240-16-6

Designed and produced by
Jerry Burman
Tel: 01803 409754

Printed in Great Britain by
CPI Antony Rowe, Chippenham, Wiltshire

Acknowledgements

This book is the product of many contributors. We owe a great debt to the participants at the 2006 INTRAC conference, particularly those who made presentations. They shared their experiences and opinions generously.

This book would not have been possible without financial support from DGIS (the Dutch Foreign Ministry) through the INTRAC Praxis Programme. This is an excellent example of a donor supporting capacity building with attitude and foresight.

We also acknowledge invaluable editorial support from INTRAC Directors, Brian Pratt and Brenda Lipson.

Contents

Introduction

'Make a habit of regularly observing the universal process of change: be assiduous in your attention to it and school yourself thoroughly in this branch of study: there is nothing more elevating to the mind.'
Marcus Aurelius[1]

Meaningless jargon?

'What *is* the work that you do?' Baffled and bemused friends frequently pose this question. We find it difficult to provide a lively and coherent response that does not leave them even more confused. How do you explain to your friends or even colleagues that you work in 'capacity building'?

The term capacity building has little meaning to those outside the narrow confines of the aid world. Even within development circles it is rarely translated into any other language, including French and Spanish. And even to English-speakers, the term capacity building conceals as much as it reveals. Few of us are sure that we know what capacity building really means. Nor are we certain that other people mean the same thing as we do. All we do know for sure is that capacity building is unquestionably a 'good thing'. After all, aid strategies are constructed around capacity building and millions of euros, pounds and dollars are invested in it. But we are left curiously dissatisfied, wondering whether capacity building is all it is made out to be.

For those working in the area of aid and development, capacity building works at many different levels – from building the capacity of a nation's economy to developing the capacity of local communities. This book focuses on the challenges of organisational capacity building in civil society and in NGOs (non government organisations). To demystify the concept of capacity building and assess its practical significance, we need to answer basic, but essential, questions:

- What is capacity building?

- Why is it so important?

- Does it work? And how do we know if it does?

---

[1] Quoted by Kaplan 2002:113

- What makes it work well sometimes? But not others?

- How well do we implement capacity building?

- What holds us back from doing it well?

- How could we improve?

Grappling with these questions begins to reveal the reality behind the jargon.

What's in it for me?

In the face of widening inequalities and relentless poverty in much of the world, there is no room for complacency. We should not spend aid money on concepts we do not really understand. No-one wants to spend their working life spouting meaningless jargon. To be effective in changing the lives of the poor and marginalised, we need to know what makes a difference.

The book explores both the theory and practice of capacity building. It highlights what we know today about both the context and concepts of capacity building. It identifies what we have learnt about good practice of capacity building. This 'theory' has emerged from experience. The text goes on to highlight what we actually do. When comparing our practice of capacity building with our professed theory, we see a worrying gap. We do not always implement what we know. Exploring why this might be, we conclude by suggesting what we can do to improve our impact.

The following pages:
1. provide an overview of contextual trends, conceptual debates and current thinking about organisational capacity building
2. assess how well the present practice measures up to this thinking
3. identify the constraining forces that inhibit implementing good practice
4. argue for essential and urgent ways forward.

This book is a companion and complement to a forthcoming INTRAC publication (*A Framework for Capacity Building* by Brenda Lipson and Martina Hunt). This volume analyses both the concepts and experiences of organisational capacity building and makes strategic recommendations for future directions. Lipson and Hunt's publication is a guide written for those responsible for designing and implementing capacity building programmes – whether with individual organisations, sectors or whole societies.

Where are we coming from?

This is aimed at anyone involved in supporting capacity building with NGOs and other civil society organisations[2] (CSOs). INTRAC believes that CSOs are key and autonomous actors for development. We acknowledge that civil society is much broader than the small number of agencies which receive funding from the aid system. Across the world, community groups, funeral societies, religious orders, leisure clubs and mass movements go back thousands of years and exist completely independent of the aid system. But the capacity building we do is usually funded from aid or from public funding. While the examples in this book are taken from the aid system, we believe that the lessons gained have relevance and application for civil society that operates without international aid support.

This publication therefore concentrates on capacity building with CSOs that receive support from the aid system in some way. It also focuses on the organisational capacity building element and makes reference to broader issues of civil society in so far as they affect capacity building. But it does not go into more conceptual issues of definitions of civil society. Those who wish to explore these important issues in more depth might look at Changing Expectations? *The Concept and Practice of Civil Society in International Development* edited by Brian Pratt.[3]

The message is that:

1. Capacity building is an internal process of change (an 'endogenous' process): the role of outsiders is to create favourable conditions and provide appropriate inputs.

2. Capacity building is a human process, profoundly affected by peoples' values and agendas. It is therefore complex, relational and political and must address human issues of motivation and interests.

3. Generic principles of good practice do exist in capacity building, but they need to be applied differently in different contexts.

4. International agencies are not doing enough to put into practice what they know.

5. We face resource and skill constraints in capacity building, but, ultimately, it is our attitudes that hold us back.

6. The way forward is to reflect on our own underlying attitudes and to have the humility, honesty, determination and courage to collaborate with others.

---

[2] The term CSO is used throughout this publication, although NGO may still be more common parlance. INTRAC believes that NGOs are critical actors in civil society, but other CSOs, such as faith-based organisations, social movements, community-based organisations, federations, trades unions and networks complement their role.

[3] www.intrac.org/publications.php?id=11

When capacity building is done well it makes a significant difference. It can make organisations more effective in achieving their mission to change lives. Good quality capacity building takes place using a variety of approaches tailored to different contexts. The following examples, from different parts of the world, reflect the diversity of capacity building interventions and highlight the positive impact capacity building can make.

The first example from Guatemala shows how some technical training for NGO staff led to war widows successfully reclaiming their land rights.

War Widows' Land Rights in Guatemala

This moving example from Guatemala demonstrates how a local NGO supported war widows to gain legal title to the land they worked. Their husbands had been massacred during the civil war in the 1980s but they had no death certificates to support their land claims. There was increasing concern that while the women had access to the land they had no legal entitlement and were thus under threat from land-grabbers or other claimants. A local NGO working in partnership with the Irish NGO, Trocaire, sponsored a team of forensic scientists to train its staff to exhume bodies and identify remains. This provided sufficient evidence to issue death certificates. In the end, 7,000 people sought legal redress through the Inter-American Court of Human Rights. After 18 months the Guatemalan courts ruled that the land had to be returned and compensation paid. A relatively modest intervention – only costing $25,000 – has had a significant long-term impact on the quality of life of many Guatemalan families.

This next example from Guyana describes a very different approach – a comprehensive donor-inspired programme with local NGOs that led to measurable changes in capacity.

Capacity Building in Guyana

Since 1997 CHF-BCCP has provided capacity building support to 20 different Guyanese NGOs, enabling them to work more effectively with local communities and offer a wide-range of services to their members and beneficiaries. CHF-BCCP provides six different types of support:

- technical assistance from a team of Canadian and Guyanese consultants
- training assistance through on-the-job training, seminars and in-house workshops
- a 'recurring costs' facility that provided additional skilled personnel for key programmes of organisations
- equipment and other assets required to enhance organisational efficiency
- assistance in undertaking networking activities and establishing affiliations
- sub-project funding assistance to expand key programmes.

Evaluations suggest that this work has generated quantitative results:

- membership of the local NGOs has increased from 19,500 to 31,870
- financial resources have increased by 300 per cent
- there has been a 45 per cent increase in the number of staff employed
- beneficiaries numbers have grown from 109,655 to 296,485 (a 170 per cent increase).

Capacity building can also transform individual and organisational behaviour. The following example from Africa shows how even quite limited, one-off inputs can contribute to a remarkable organisational change processes.

Organisational Transformation

Riven by division and corruption, the Tangababwe Evangelical Fellowship (TEF – not its real name) existed only in name. Its Chair and Vice Chair were receiving gifts from the country's President in exchange for political support. TEF had lost all credibility with its members and donors had long-since departed. However, a 'last chance' capacity building workshop breathed new life into an all-but-dead organisation. The leadership and membership emotionally admitted their faults, forgave each other and had a renewed vision for the organisation. After this they worked together to develop a new more socially-relevant strategy. Participants pledged sufficient finance to cover six month's operating costs. TEF made a public apology to other churches for its past behaviour. Soon afterwards, TEF brought these same churches together to advocate together for revision of the national constitution.

These three cases illustrate distinct approaches to capacity building. These range from technical assistance and training, to funding overheads or core costs, to facilitating meetings out of which new strategies and activities are generated.

Clearly there are many examples of such initiatives world-wide, but unfortunately surprisingly few of them are written up as case studies or published with evidence of impact. Most of our information about the impact of capacity building is anecdotal. We hear stories of remarkable change, but there is little formal research or body of literature to support this.

Why now?

Civil society capacity building is at a critical juncture. Capacity building has been enjoying a 'golden age'. Donors have invested considerable sums of money in capacity building and it remains a strategic priority for many (DAC 2006, Morgan 2006 – see Chapter 2). Yet despite these massive aid flows, poverty is increasing in the poorest parts of Africa. In Asia and Latin America there are widening inequalities, where many of the poor are untouched by the benefits of 'exclusionary' economic growth. Capacity building is not delivering hoped-for results. Donors are also questioning the importance of civil society in development. The 'golden age' is already looking tarnished. As a result, all of us involved in capacity building work must reflect on past practice and adapt our work accordingly.

Anyone engaged in building the capacity of civil society understands that it is essential that our work makes a genuine difference to the poor. The poor cannot afford the luxury of costly and confused aid programmes.

We need to question our own understanding of capacity building. We should not shy away from facing up to hard truths where programmes have failed. How can we learn and improve our practice? What should we do differently in the future? But we should also highlight and document all those experiences that have gone well. We should celebrate positive outcomes, rather than dwell on problems. This provides valuable evidence that capacity building can make a difference.

There is still space to be creative in capacity building, but it is contracting. There are more constraints and restrictions that limit our freedom of action. As a result we must think and act before it is too late. To help facilitate and promote this process, INTRAC organised an international conference on capacity building in December 2006. This book is the product of that conference. The deliberations and discussions are interwoven in the text of this book. A summary report of the 2006 Conference can be downloaded from: www.intrac.org/pages/CBprogramme.html

---

INTRAC Capacity Building Conference

The International Conference on Civil Society and Capacity Building took place in Oxford, UK in December 2006. A hundred and fifty development practitioners from 49 countries gathered to explore some of the key challenges faced by those committed to civil society capacity building. A range of papers were presented and the participants contributed to rigorous and searching discussions on the key issues facing those engaged in and funding capacity building. INTRAC had prepared a number of papers for this conference, including an overview paper entitled, 'Unsettling Times for Civil Society Capacity Building' (Hailey and James 2006); a draft review of the contextual changes 'Capacity Building in the Context of New Aid Effectiveness' by Sen and Pratt; a consolidation of practitioner learning from the Praxis Programme 'Investigating the Mystery of Capacity Building' (James and Wrigley 2006); and a survey of International NGO approaches entitled 'Taking stock – a snapshot of INGO engagement in civil society capacity building' (Lipson and Warren 2006). All but Sen and Pratt can be accessed at www.intrac.org/pages/CBprogramme.html

---

Where will we go?

Part One of the book deals with the context and the concept of capacity building. Chapter 1 starts by reaffirming that capacity building is a confused and contested concept. Definitions remain elastic. Yet a consensus on capacity building is emerging. Diverse stakeholders agree that capacity building is an internal process of complex human change. Outsiders can cultivate or catalyse, but not control, capacity building. We see such emphases echoed by recent developments in business management theory. Chapter 2 places capacity building in the wider aid context. It describes how capacity building is still a priority in aid flows. It goes on to analyse how recent shifts in the global context are affecting civil society capacity building.

Part Two identifies what we have learnt about the elements of good capacity building practice. There is increasing agreement about what works well in practice. We know what tends to work better and what generally fails. Chapter 3 shows that capacity building is fundamentally a human change process. Effective capacity building is therefore people-centred, addresses issues of power and relationship and encourages individuals to take responsibility for their own change process. Chapter 4 analyses the importance of locally appropriate provision of capacity building services. It highlights the value of using a variety of methods and adapting them to particular contexts and cultures. It also emphasises the importance of working with local providers of such services. Chapter 5 addresses good practice planning and management of capacity building. It shows that to be effective we need to implement both a coherent and contextualised strategy. It also highlights the importance of appropriate funding support, and monitoring and evaluation.

Part Three explores the reality of current capacity building practice. It examines uncomfortable, but important, questions: how well are development agencies living up to their own standards in capacity building? Chapter 6 compares what we know about capacity building with what international agencies actually do. In many cases agencies are not implementing the good practice principles. We accept unrealistic and instant expectations of highly complex processes. We design programmes around donor priorities, not the interests of those they are intended to help. Chapter 7 explores the reasons for our failure to implement what we know. It highlights constraints that arise from the aid context. It also shows there is a lack of resources and skills. Ultimately, however, it concludes that the underlying factor is stakeholders' lack of commitment to overcome their inherent self-interest.

Part Four looks to the future. Chapter 8 identifies how to move forward from our current impasse, our need to address contextual constraints at a policy level, the resource constraints for donors, the skill constraints of capacity building providers and the lack of motivation from CSOs. For each actor involved, it involves making changes at a much tougher and deeper level and putting into practice the humility, honesty, discipline and courage to make capacity building effective. Chapter 9 summarises the book and points out potential challenges as the economic, political, social and technical environment for capacity building changes in the future.

PART 1

The Context and Concept of Capacity Building

To improve our practice of capacity building we must first understand more about the concept itself. Amidst the complexities, jargon and diverse interpretations we need to establish common reference points. There is an encouraging, emerging consensus amongst diverse stakeholders about the concept of capacity building. Interestingly, the commercial management field is starting to reflect recent thinking about experience generated by the aid system over many years.

But we also know that capacity building is profoundly influenced by the context in which it operates. We will explore how current changes in the global aid context are affecting capacity building – both in terms of capacity building needs and the nature of support given.

CHAPTER 1

From Confusion to Consensus: The Concept of Capacity Building

'The concept of capacity and its practice remain puzzling, confusing and even vacuous especially in international development'.
Peter Morgan 2006:3

'Aid agencies would be wise to have no truck with the new jargon of "capacity building" and to insist on using language and terms that have identifiable and precise meanings'.
Mick Moore 1995

The World Bank's recent evaluation of its capacity building work points out a major anomaly. At the same time as claiming that 50 per cent of its disbursements are related to capacity building, the Bank also admits it has no accepted definition (2006). Many international NGOs would fare no better. Despite the on-going commitment to capacity building we are not clear what we mean by the concept. Definitions remain elastic. The fact that different stakeholders have different interpretations obviously gives rise to misunderstandings and confusion.

This chapter outlines the diverse meanings ascribed to capacity building. It shows how different stakeholders pursue capacity building for different, and not always mutually inclusive, purposes. Yet it appears there is a recent convergence of opinion from a variety of sources leading to an emerging consensus about what capacity building is. Recent emphases in management and organisational theory in the public and private sectors reinforce this emerging consensus, as do shifts in donor aid thinking.

Conceptual Elasticity

Capacity building is a prime example of jargon that can conceal more than it reveals. There is no tight, internationally-accepted definition of capacity building. Consequently, no one can be quite sure what others mean by it. This causes confusion within and between agencies. But because people feel that they ought to know, they rarely probe to ensure they are talking about the same thing. This confusion is exacerbated because the term capacity building is not readily translated into other languages. Indeed, in most countries, the English term is used, 'as if to emphasise the concept's esoteric character' (Sterland 2006).

Our understanding of capacity building has been dominated by institutional and organisational thinking rooted in the cultures of North America and Europe. But even so there is a marked diversity of interpretations and definitions. For example, in France capacity building is seen to be more about individuals and processes and they perceive Anglophone capacity building as focusing more on organisations and results (Sorgenfrei 2004). Despite the lack of an internationally-accepted definition, much of the research has focused on the technical and practical aspects of capacity building. As a result, the role of capacity building in shaping meaning or influencing our understanding of development has been underplayed. There is possibility that capacity building as a culturally-influenced concept 'rooted in a particular ideology and way of thinking' has been ignored or overlooked (Sen & Pratt, 2006).

Definitional vagueness allows different stakeholders to ascribe their own meaning to capacity building and interpret it, unchallenged, from their own perspective. This means some see capacity building as unquestionably positive – like 'motherhood' and 'apple pie' - impossible to disagree with. For others, however, it is intrinsically negative. In Iran, for example, the government sees capacity building as 'bad' (Squire 2006). This is because in many places capacity building is seen as a foreign, Anglophone concept that automatically connotes values of Western political democracy. Here, capacity building is seen as part of an internationally-determined, donor development discourse.

So despite repeated calls for greater agreement on meaning, capacity building remains a nebulous concept – 'broad, contested, ambiguous, and imprecise' (James and Wrigley 2007:3). There are strong incentives to keep it that way. Its elasticity allows different stakeholders to stretch it to mean whatever they need it to mean. Peter Morgan points out that for many donors: 'the operational utility of the concept actually comes from its ambiguity and lack of boundaries' (2006:6). A wide diversity of hard-to-fund development initiatives can be re-packaged, re-labelled and re-legitimised under this all-encompassing term.

Such flexibility is only possible because capacity building, as a concept, is not supported by an accepted and tested body of theory and lacks academic rigour (ibid.). Only two universities, in Canada and in Germany, teach courses focusing on capacity building. There is no obvious professional association or network promoting, validating or accrediting this work or developing a code of practice for practitioners.

The question 'What is capacity building?' is therefore the source of much debate, and reflected in varied discourses (Eade 1999, Green and Battcock 2003, Lusthaus et. al., 1999, Fukuda-Parr et. al. 2002, Black 2003). To some it is a process of building various institutional capacities, to others a way of describing what capacities best add value in the development process. Others see it is the accumulation of social capital, while some describe it as an ideological position. The text box below illustrates the diversity of perspectives:

What is Capacity Building: A Definitional List

- helping locate the organisation in the wider world
- facilitating an institution to design and deliver policies
- developing an organisation's ability to satisfy or influence its stakeholders
- developing an organisation's autonomy and independence
- enabling an institution to create value
- a collation of institutional strengthening capital
- building organisational or managerial strengths
- enhancing ability to evolve and adapt to change
- opening the organisation to innovations and new ideas
- transferring knowledge and new learning
- developing core skills and competencies
- empowering staff and volunteers
- changing patterns of behaviour
- improving morale, enhancing motivation and reducing stress and anxiety.

Not surprisingly then for international NGOs (INGOs) capacity building remains subject to 'continued conceptual muddiness' (Lipson and Warren 2006:15). The lack of framework for analysis has allowed a multiplicity of meanings and interpretations to emerge. The text box below illustrates the wide variety of INGO definitions.

INGO Understanding of Capacity Building

In response to the question: What do you understand by 'capacity building' 63 INGOs responded:

- 20 per cent had no formal or standardised definitions
- 55 per cent had shorter statements linked to improved performance of partners
- 25 per cent had complex statements which included references to the nature of the process, the goals pursued, the type of organisations they worked with and the kinds of activities undertaken.

Source: Lipson and Warren 2006

There are also a wide variety of terms used to describe the concept. Capacity building is the most commonly used term, yet many commentators do not like it because it implies a simple, mechanical process, done by outside 'builders'. They prefer such terms as 'capacity development, strengthening, enhancement or even capacity cultivation. More important than the terminology is the understanding that underpins it. Although we share the reservations about the use of the term 'capacity building', we accept that it is the most commonly used phrase. We will therefore continue to use it in this book. We would prefer to fight for the understanding of the concept and practice than squabble over the label used.

Whichever term is used, it is important that there is some degree of shared understanding. But as the following example from a large UK NGO (which we shall call TINGO) illustrates, this process can be difficult and elusive. Despite having gone to great lengths to reach a common agreement about their approach to capacity building ten years ago, a recent TINGO evaluation found there was now little shared understanding among current staff. Management had failed to maintain staff awareness and learning systems in the face of staff turnover.

TINGO's Understanding of Capacity Building

As early as 1996, TINGO had agreed a definition of capacity building: *'Capacity building is a tailor-made process to strengthen partner organisations and which seeks to enhance their effectiveness and impact on the poor in relation to their mission, context and resources. Capacity building must involve openness to a two-way process which involves TINGO reflecting and leaning how it can improve its support and partnerships'.*

Using this definition, TINGO had successfully developed a capacity building strategy. This was supported by a series of briefing papers and operational manuals which outlined the rationale, principles, approach, model, explanations, funding strategies and relationship with donors.

But despite all this effort, a review of TINGO's capacity building work in 2006, found that most staff were still unclear what TINGO meant by capacity building. As a result, there was no consistency in coding capacity building initiatives into TINGO's database or records. Staff had virtually no knowledge of the manuals or strategy documents. They could not be located in the official files as they had been relegated to an unused store-cupboard.

Contested Purposes – Capacity building for what?

Not only is there no universally accepted definition of capacity building, but there is also limited agreement on its role and purpose. There are number of reasons for investing in capacity building. The text box below outlines some of them. They highlight the differing interests and agendas of key stakeholders, which are not always complementary.

Why Build Capacity: Common Purposes
- enhance ability to deliver services or programmes
- increase accountability and greater legitimacy
- increase productivity and improve efficiency and effectiveness
- increase levels of participation in decision-making and implementation
- pass on technical skills
- build community involvement and mobilise communities to meet their own needs
- develop greater solidarity in the community and mobilise action
- embrace innovation and being open to new approaches or technologies
- promote viable and sustainable social enterprise
- facilitate sense making and promoting greater understanding of the operational context.

Despite the plethora of explanations as to the purpose of capacity building it is possible to differentiate between them. We identify four general purposes of capacity building:

- **a social/political purpose:** promoting societal and democratic change, increased levels of participation in decision-making and implementation

- **an instrumental purpose:** improving development project implementation, results and accountabilities

- **an organisational purpose:** improving development organisations' sustainability, autonomy, integrity, independence and resilience

- **a transformational purpose:** shifting relationships and power dynamics.

Experience suggests that the attitude and assumptions on which these approaches rest will dictate which one is adopted. For example, those who believe that capacity building must deliver quick, measurable results and can be achieved through the simple transfer of skills, will favour a more instrumental approach. Those who believe that capacity building requires a change in power relationships will take a transformational approach.

The target or focus of capacity building initiatives also varies considerably. Capacity building initiatives can be aimed at different target groups. There is a broad spectrum of capacity building targets.

| Individual | Group | Single Organisation | Network | Societal |

These vary from helping a specific individual to develop him/herself at one end of the spectrum to facilitating community and organisational change in the middle or promoting societal change at the other end of the spectrum. While all these are inter-related, it is clear that the priorities of different stakeholders will influence which are prioritised.

Eade (1997:35) usefully outlined some of these issues in the form of a matrix which recognises the difference between capacity building in NGOs and civil society. It distinguishes between capacity building as a means to an end, as a process and as an end in itself.

	Capacity building as means	Capacity building as process	Capacity building as ends
Capacity building in the NGO	Strengthen organisation to perform specified **activities**	Process of reflection, leadership, inspiration, adaptation and search for greater **coherence** between NGO mission, structure and activities	Strengthen NGO to survive and fulfil its **mission** as defined by the organisation
Capacity building in civil society	Strengthen capacity of primary stakeholders to implement defined **activities**	Fostering **communication:** processes of debate, relationship building, conflict resolution and improved ability of society to deal with difference	Strengthen capacity of primary stakeholders to participate in political and socio-economic arena according to **objectives** defined by them

The cost of confusion

The resulting lack of a common frame of reference is not an abstract problem for it has significant operational implications for international development agencies as they implement and manage capacity building projects. As Morgan probes: 'International development agencies harmonising their approaches in a sector wide approach (SWAp) to support capacity development means coordinating to do what exactly? Strategies for capacity development add up to a focus on what activities?' (2006:2). The confused nature of capacity building leaves it open to abuse – with different stakeholders using it for their own ends.

The lack of agreement within, and between, different development agencies means that there is little shared understanding, and limited exploration of the concepts and values underpinning effective capacity building. Such definitional confusion is well exemplified in this example from the International Federation of the Red Cross and Red Crescent Societies (IFRC).

Conceptual Confusions

INGO confusion is well reflected in the IFRC's Policy Document on Co-operation for Capacity Building. In the space of a few pages two distinct views of capacity building were articulated.

- *'to improve the ability and capacity of National Societies to develop and make the most efficient use of new and available resources to achieve the humanitarian aims of the Movement in a sustainable way'.*

- *'to improve the ability and capacities of communities, families and individuals to become less vulnerable and enjoy fuller and more productive lives'.*

While both definitions are worthwhile and laudable they reflect a strategic tension in the Red Cross/Red Crescent Movement. Should it focus its capacity building at the organisational level (i.e. the National Society and its staff) or should the societal level (developing individuals and institutions in the wider community) be the priority? Although these are complementary rather than contradictory goals, it begs the question as to where best they should target their limited capacity building resources. This is a question that has dogged the Red Cross/Red Crescent for the last fifteen years.

The failure to define capacity building also makes it impossible to judge performance. If we do not clearly define the goal, we are never able to say whether we have been successful or failed. It also undermines the potential for learning, as the 2006 INGO Survey illustrates:

'A primary concern may be a resulting lack of consistency and coherence in the capacity building work undertaken by different units within the INGO. Learning opportunities may be reduced without common conceptual, definitional and methodological references. Articulation and dissemination of experiences may also tend to remain at the "micro" case study level. All of this may have a "knock on" implication for the level of debate and discussion on capacity building within the sector as a whole'
(Lipson and Warren 2006:3).

This conceptual confusion also undermines the potential for stakeholders to work together in capacity building. Because many are not clear what they mean by capacity building, nor explicit about why they are supporting it, this makes it difficult to collaborate effectively.

There is also tension between practitioners concerned with solving immediate problems or challenges (financial crises, team conflicts, systems failures, structural dysfunctionality, leadership problems, etc), and the interest of more cerebral commentators trying to get behind these issues, assess their root causes or determine their wider meaning. Unfortunately, these two groups do not always meet physically or conceptually.

A coherent consensus?

It appears, however, that amidst the confusion, hope is in sight. Greater conceptual coherence is emerging. Despite the ongoing debates as to role and purpose of capacity building, there is an underlying agreement that capacity building is about change – making things better, adding value and developing new assets or talents. It is also about how best to develop new capabilities (i.e. institutional assets or collective skills) and new competencies (i.e. individual skills and energy or new personal behaviours).

The most common usage of the term capacity, associates it with action i.e. the 'ability to' or 'power to' do. Capacity may be expressed in different forms, such as:

- *Human capabilities*, for example, attributes that can be found in individuals, their skills, knowledge, experience, values and attitudes.
- *Relational capabilities*, for example, shared value or belief systems, networks of groups or organisations with a common cause, sharing information.
- *Resource capabilities*, for example, tangible resources such as money, buildings and computers or, intangible resources such as time and knowledge.

Recent definitions of capacity

'The ability of individuals, institutions and societies to perform functions, solve problems and set and achieve objectives in a sustainable manner'
(UNDP 2006:3)

'Capacity is the ability of people, organisations and society as a whole to manage their affairs successfully. Capacity development is the process whereby people, organisations and society as a whole unleash, strengthen, create adapt and maintain capacity over time'
(DAC 2006:5)

'Capacity is that emergent combination of attributes that enables a human system to create developmental value'
(Morgan 2006:8)

In attempting to invest the concept with more operational content, there are important emerging areas of conceptual congruence. These are illustrated by the publications of a diverse range of stakeholders on capacity building in the last twelve months: official agencies (UNDP 2006, DAC 2006); academic writers (Morgan 2006, Fowler 2006, Eyben 2006); international NGOs (Lipson and Warren 2006) and capacity building practitioners (James and Wrigley 2007). Such consensus is reinforcing shifts in thinking in the broader, commercial management field.

There is general agreement that capacity building:

- is a **complex, human process based on values, emotions, and beliefs**. Change is often motivated by 'personal' factors. The UNDP document talks about the need to analyse core issues from a human development perspective (2006:10). The DAC report also emphasises the importance of leadership in inspiring change (2006).

- is an **internal process (endogenous – 'formed from within') that involves the main actor taking responsibility** for the process of change. According to UNDP, capacity development is 'a primarily endogenous and domestically driven process' (ibid.:3) - though this does not preclude learning from outside. Similarly, Sida's manual for capacity development argues that 'capacity development must grow from the inside. Growth of this type can benefit from receiving stimulation externally, but it cannot be developed by outsiders'. (Bergstrom 2005:39). Outsiders can only facilitate, not provide, capacity building.

- involves shifts in **power** and **identity** – capacity involves 'people acting together to take control over their own lives' (Morgan 2006:7). UNDP states that capacity development is an inherently political process (2006:3) that challenges existing power dynamics.

- involves **changes in relationship between elements of open-systems**. Eyben points out that 'complexity theory posits that self-organising sets of relationships ... are a key element in societal change'. She asserts that 'the dynamics of relations shape peoples' behaviour'(2006:4). This fits with Morgan's description of capacity as a 'collective ability' (2006:7).

- is **uncertain and unpredictable** to a degree. UNDP points out that 'Capacity development is a complex process that cannot be rushed and outcomes cannot be expected to evolve in a controlled and linear fashion' (2006:3). Sida reinforces such thinking by showing that 'capacity development involves a gradual change that rarely follows a straight, clearly staked out route'. (Bergstrom 2005:39) Morgan describes capacity as a latent or potential state (ibid.). Many stakeholders now appreciate we cannot control what will happen in a living system, we can only disturb it. Managing this process well, however, can help steer it in the right direction.

- is **contextual**. Capacity building needs and solutions are powerfully influenced by the culture and the changing context – the politics, economy, social, religious, ethnic, class, environment and history. Capacity building will be different in different places. As UNDP states 'It is about achieving "best fit" in a particular situation'. (2006)

This consensus is both striking and encouraging. Diverse stakeholders are now in agreement about the concept of capacity building. The principle of 'triangulation' posits that if the same information comes from a variety of sources, it is more likely to be correct. This conceptual coherence is also supported by recent shifts in organisation and management thinking from other sectors. This provides welcome validation from a different angle.

Thinking in organisational capacity building has been influenced by developments in management research generally. This is reflected in the interest in the resource-based view of strategy. This view asserts that an organisation's ability to add value by the way it works is crucial to its long-term success and sustainability (Barney 2006, Morgan 2006). The emphasis on strategic positioning and strategic planning which dominated much manage-ment thinking in the 1990s has been replaced by an awareness of the importance of specific organisational competencies. It argues that organisational success depends on developing hard-to-imitate attributes and capacities. These might include organisational values, collec-tive knowledge or trust, personal behaviours, competencies or expertise that is unique to a certain group or team. The implication is that we should focus on developing such capaci-ties as talent (the ability of an organisation to attract, motivate and retain skilled employ-ees); shared mindset (confidence in a shared identity and organisational culture); agility and flexibility (the ability to respond to and manage change) and learning and knowledge (the ability to apply knowledge, creativity and innovation).

Furthermore, there is much greater appreciation and understanding of the role of personal values or beliefs in organisational life. As the text box below highlights, researchers have increasingly emphasised the role of such factors as emotional intelligence and spiritual dimensions in determining management effectiveness or shaping organisations culture.

Recent emphases in Management Thinking

The centrality of values

In different ways such leading management thinkers and researchers as Adair (2002) and Collins and Porras (1997) have also emphasised the importance of values in organisational sustainability and change. Influential longitudinal research by Collins and Porras in 1997 on 18 visionary companies that had been leaders in their industries for 50 years, showed that their success was due to focusing on non-economic values and an empowering culture. They actually outperformed their competitors by as much as 16:1 (Korac-Kakabadse et al., 2002: 165). Management thinking is now concentrating on values-driven change processes.

A spiritual dimension to organisational behaviour

Management writers have also given increased attention to the spiritual dimension of organisational behaviour. Some observe an 'explosion of interest in spirituality as a new dimension of management. The present spiritual trend is probably the most significant trend in management since the 1950s.' (Howard 2002:230) Organisational consultants and popular writers such as John Adair, Peter Senge, Tom Peters, Peter Vaill, Steven Covey, Charles Handy and Harrison Owen are increasingly explicit about the spiritual dimension to organisational life. Wagner-Marsh and Conley highlight a number of Fortune 100 firms which 'all have a spiritual dimension to leadership and management development programmes' (1999:294).

Emotional intelligence in leadership

Emotional intelligence describes one's innate ability to feel, use, understand and learn from your own emotions and those of others and of groups. In other words your capacity to recognise your own feelings (and those of others) and the way they impact on your behaviour or work. Increasingly evidence suggests that many effective leaders or managers display high levels of 'emotional intelligence', and their performance is determined by their emotional maturity and ability to mobilise their emotional intelligence (Goleman, 2000). Effective leaders demonstrate high levels of self-awareness, are capable of self-management, are socially aware and well able to manage a diverse range of relationships.

Conclusion

Operational incentives to keep the concept of capacity building elastic and ambiguous result in poor communication, confusion and reduced impact. If we fail to develop shared understanding at the outset of a capacity building programme, then the process is likely to be marred by misunderstandings and tensions. There may be disagreements about the methods to use or even in whether the intervention was successful or not.

The good news is that there is an emerging conceptual coherence, at least on paper. Diverse stakeholders are largely in agreement that capacity building:

- is a **complex, human** process
- is an **internal** process

- involves changes in **relationship** between elements of open-systems and is therefore uncertain and unpredictable
- involves shifts in **power** and **identity**

This has significant implications for capacity building practice as we shall see in Chapters 3–5.

The reality is that capacity building is a dynamic process. It may at times be messy and counter-intuitive. To a degree that is only to be expected in any creative and evolving process. It surfaces powerful human drivers of self-interest. It is an organic, living process. As such the metaphor of cultivating capacity, rather than building it, may shed more light. It is a conscious approach to promoting change, which, if taken seriously, has very radical and far-reaching implications not only for skills and behaviours, but also power dynamics within and between individuals and organisations.

Capacity building, however, is not just a conceptual idea. It involves practical action, which takes place in a specific context and is highly influenced by it. To understand better the concept of capacity building we therefore have to know about its context. The next chapter explores some of the current contextual changes affecting capacity building.

CHAPTER 2

Challenge and Control: The Changing Context of Capacity Building

'It is not rocket science to say that context is everything, and yet in judging NGOs, most observers ignore it almost entirely'
Hailey and Smillie (2000:161)

Capacity building is deeply affected by the context in which it operates. It does not take place in 'laboratory conditions' – a sanitised vacuum with controlled variables. It occurs in a noisy, congested and rapidly changing global environment. Contextual issues, such as the global economy, power relations, political, technological or social matters, influence both donor support for civil society as well as for building of its capacity. Analysis of other capacity-building interventions has clearly demonstrated, 'the profound and far-reaching influence which the different contexts had'. (James 2001:124)

The aid context for capacity building is currently in a state of flux. Orthodoxies that prevailed ten years ago are now being questioned. The aid policy decisions recently taken by some donors raise significant strategic challenges for those of us working in CSO capacity building. Obviously we do not know the extent to which these policy statements will be applied consistently across the globe. Implementation of policy is never quite as black and white as it appears in Northern pronouncements. Some donors may stand out against the prevailing tides. But it is likely that these shifts will have a considerable impact on our capacity building work. We would do well to be ready by understanding what is happening in the wider context, what is changing and what has not.

This chapter highlights the influence of poverty on the role and importance of capacity building. To appreciate the potential and limitations of capacity building, we need to recognise the generic shortage of resources in poor communities.

The second section provides evidence of the current interest in capacity building and the way it has grown over the years. This is reflected in the way agencies and INGOs support and promote capacity building and the range of new organisations in the North and the South established to support it.

The third section goes on to identify some aid trends that may have a direct impact on capacity building. Shifts such as the reaffirmation of the role of the state in development; donor harmonisation and increased alignment of aid with foreign policy may be constricting the space for civil society capacity building.

The Challenges of Poverty

At the start of the new millennium, the world's governments united to make a remarkable promise to the victims of global poverty. They presented a bold vision to 'free our fellow men, women and children from abject and dehumanising conditions of extreme poverty'. However, the 2005 UNDP Human Development report graphically describes how 'the promise to the world's poor is being broken' (2005:3). Rich country trade policies continue to deny poor countries and poor people a fair share of global prosperity. Violent conflict blights the lives of hundreds of millions of people (ibid.)

> *'While there are pockets of improvement, the overall report card on progress makes for depressing reading. Human development is faltering in some key areas and already deep inequalities are widening... We live in a divided world. In 2003, 18 countries with a combined population of 460 million registered lower scores on the human development index than in 1990... In the midst of an increasingly prosperous global economy, 10.7 million people do not live to see their 5th birthday. More than 1 billion people survive on less than $1 per day. Yet a fifth of the world live in countries where many people think nothing of spending $2 a day on a cappuccino. Today someone in Zambia has less chance of reaching the age of 30, than someone born in England in 1840 – and the gap is widening.'*
>
> *Nelson Mandela said in 2005, 'Massive poverty and obscene inequality are such terrible scourges of our times – times in which the world boast breathtaking advances in science, technology, industry and wealth accumulation – that they have to rank alongside apartheid and slavery as social evils'.*
> (ibid pp 3-5)

The challenges of poverty, humanitarian emergencies, and on-going conflict make capacity building even more challenging. This is powerfully illustrated by HIV/AIDS, the pandemic which has inflicted the single greatest reversal in human development (ibid. 3). This has profound direct and indirect effects on capacity building. For example, in many parts of sub-Saharan Africa, local CSOs are experiencing growing rates of staff sickness and death. Increasingly, staff are absent caring for sick relatives or attending funerals. In such a draining context, it may be more appropriate to have goals of capacity maintenance and organisational survival, rather than unrealistic expectations of dramatic progress.

How HIV affects CSOs

Research undertaken in Malawi, Uganda and Tanzania in 2005 revealed that at least one staff member had died of AIDS in more than 60 per cent of responding CSOs. More than 70 per cent believed some of their staff were HIV positive. HIV/AIDS leads to rising medical, funeral and pension costs for CSOs. Having staff infected by HIV and affected by AIDS in the extended family also leads to a loss in productivity. There is increasing absenteeism due to sickness, care of the ill and funerals. In Malawi, staff estimate they spend more than 14 working days per year attending funerals. Scarce management time is being diverted to dealing with HIV/AIDS issues. CSOs are silently struggling with concurrent problems of increasing overheads and declining performance. The research estimated that HIV was currently increasing staff bills by seven per cent per year and reducing staff time at work by ten per cent per annum. It should be noted that these countries have much lower HIV prevalence than Botswana, Lesotho, Namibia, South Africa, Swaziland, Zambia and Zimbabwe.

Taken from James, R, 2006

Capacity building for CSOs is also adversely affected by the international market for labour – the flow of skills away from poor countries. An imperfect international job market, richly rewards local staff who can leave their country for an international posting. The World Bank estimates that about 70,000 highly qualified professionals and experts leave Africa every year (2006). According to the International Organisation for Migration, Ethiopia lost 75 per cent of its skilled workforce between 1980 and 1991 (Tebeje 2005). For CSOs, many of their best staff are offered powerful incentives to leave local civil society, either to work abroad or to join the donor world.

Poverty therefore has a major direct and indirect impact on capacity building, but in diametrically opposed ways. Poverty is both the major driver for capacity building and the major constraint on its success. The poorer the context, the more capacity building is needed but the harder it is to achieve.

On-going interest and donor investment in capacity building

The need for capacity building support is not being questioned. Documents from the early 1990s show how official (bi-lateral and multi-lateral) donors prioritised capacity building (Rondinelli 1989, Johnston and Wohgemuth 1993, James 1994). Both budgets and policy statements today reflect unrelenting donor interest in capacity building.

Official estimates are that a quarter of total development aid, $15 billion a year, is ostensibly spent on capacity building – although obviously this depends on how capacity building is defined (DAC 2006). The World Bank labelled capacity building the 'missing link in development' (Morgan 2006:3).

The primary role of capacity building is also well-illustrated in Sida's mission statement and policy on capacity development.

Sida Policy for Capacity Development (2000)

Sida's task is to make sustainable development possible. Our principal method is capacity and institutional development (taken from Sida's mission statement 1995).

Sida shall increase its support for capacity development in partner countries to:

- develop the knowledge and competence of individuals and organisations
- develop organisations and/or/systems of organisations
- change and strengthen institutional frameworks in the form of policies and laws and/or informal norms which stipulate the limits within which individuals and organisations develop.

International NGOs (INGOs) are also consistent in their support for capacity building. INTRAC's longitudinal research on INGOs and capacity building conducted in 1994, 1998 and 2006 suggests that more than 90 per cent of responding international NGOs are actively engaged in capacity building work (James 1994; James et. al. 1998; Lipson and Warren 2006). The 2006 survey found that 65 per cent of responding INGOs have a specific programme which is solely dedicated to civil society capacity building. While 45 per cent estimated that they spend almost one-third of their overall programme funds on capacity building,[4] 72 per cent of responding INGOs said they had capacity building or civil society strengthening specialists in their organisations. Such findings demonstrate the continued emphasis that most INGOs place on their capacity building work.

Capacity building has become an essential part of the current development scene. It is reflected in the number of new organisations (NGOs and social enterprises, policy centres and think-tanks) established around the world in the last 20 years. In Africa, Asia and Eastern Europe, a wide variety of civil society capacity building providers have emerged, such as CDRA (South Africa) CDRN (Uganda); CABUNGO (Malawi); EASUN (Tanzania) Centre InterBilim (Central Asia); MCIC (Macedonia), Civic Initiatives (Serbia), NPO Network (China), Zenid (Jordan) and PNGO (Palestine). In 1996 the International Forum of Capacity Building was started to bring a much-needed Southern voice to the internationally-dominated discourse.

International Forum on Capacity Building

In 1996, three Southern NGO representatives to the NGO Working Group of the World Bank established the International Forum on Capacity Building (ICBF). The aim was to ensure a Southern voice in setting the capacity building agenda. At the time capacity building processes and programmes were largely driven by Northern stakeholders from official and INGO agencies. This group was initially chaired by PRIA from India. They prepared regional and then a global synthesis report on Southern NGO capacity building issues and priorities. They hosted a series of multi-stakeholder dialogue workshops in Brussels and Washington. In recent years, however, IFCB has suffered from problems of its own leadership transition away from PRIA as secretariat. This has been compounded by declining donor interest as key donor staff have shifted jobs.

---

[4] It is likely that this is an over-estimate. Some respondents used such a broad definition of capacity building that it incorporated what others would describe as partnerships. One evaluation which Rick James carried out for an INGO in 2006, revealed that mis-coding in budgets had led them to exaggerate their investment in capacity building by 33%.

International NGOs have also emerged in the last 20 years to support the capacity building priority. INTRAC was started in 1991 to support NGOs and CSOs by exploring policy issues and by strengthening management and organisational effectiveness. The European Centre for Development Policy Management (ECDPM) was created in 1986 to reinforce the capacities of public, private and non-profit organisations in ACP countries. In North America, the Impact Alliance was formed in 2001 as an international partnership advancing social change through capacity development. It promotes collaborative learning, innovation and social entrepreneurship.

As well as on-going investment, it is also clear that over the last decade donor understanding of capacity building has developed. In 2006 alone there were four major donor studies of capacity building:

- The World Bank carried out an extensive evaluation of its support to 'Capacity Building in Africa' (2006).

- The Development Assistance Committee of the Organisation for Economic Co-operation and Development (DAC/OECD 2006) consolidated their learning in a paper entitled: 'The Challenge of Capacity Development: Working Towards Good Practice'.

- The ECDPM has also done some complementary and important work in their 'Study on Capacity, Change and Performance' releasing a series of insightful papers (such as 'The Concept of Capacity' Morgan, P. 2006)

- UNDP published a useful 'Capacity Development Practice Note' (2006). This paper provides UNDP staff with a basic understanding of capacity issues; why capacity development is important and how best to support it. This paper also identified ten 'default' principles for good capacity building practice that are well worth noting:

UNDP Ten Principles for Capacity Development

The UNDP promotes ten principles that inspire ownership, transfigure leadership and help ensure progress in capacity development efforts:

1. don't rush: capacity development is a long-term process
2. respect the value systems and foster self-esteem
3. scan locally and globally; reinvent locally
4. challenge mindsets and power differentials
5. think and act in terms of sustainable capacity outcomes
6. establish positive incentives
7. integrate external inputs into national priorities, processes and systems
8. build on existing capacities rather than create new ones
9. stay engaged under difficult circumstances
10. remain accountable to ultimate beneficiaries

Recent research has also highlighted the way that the capacity building work of INGOs has evolved. Comparison of the INTRAC studies of INGO approaches to capacity building undertaken in 1994, 1998 and 2006, reveals significant developments. For example, INGOs now have:

- more in-depth, complex definitions of capacity building; clearer strategies integrating their capacity building work and increasingly identify multiple levels of interventions and target groups in novel ways

- a longer-term perspective: 30 per cent of respondents now take a five-year time perspective for their programmatic work

- more knowledge about good practice and greater awareness of the potential impact of effective capacity building work (in 1998 few INGOs appeared to have any appreciation of what constituted good practice or its impact).

The latest survey results also suggests that 'there are now about 25 per cent of respondents who take a nuanced approach to capacity building' (Lipson and Warren 2006: 44). The authors suggest such agencies appear to have a real understanding of the complexities of capacity building work, and the concepts and practices involved. This includes a greater understanding of how context affects capacity building. As a result they now implement capacity building differently from the past and work with a broader range of different types of CSOs including community-based organisations and networks (rather than simply NGOs).

Constricting Civil Society Space

There are also, however, important changes in the aid context that are undermining capacity building of civil society. Shifts in the global aid architecture are posing further challenges for capacity building of civil society. Sen and Pratt (2006) highlight a number of significant changes that will have direct consequences for civil society capacity building. These include:

i.   reaffirmation of the role of the state in development
ii. greater donor harmonisation
iii. the ongoing alignment of aid with foreign policy
iv. renewed donor emphasis on economic growth rather than poverty alleviation.

Privatisation as the aid agenda of the 1980s and 1990s, which endowed civil society with a more significant development role, has been replaced by state-centred policies. While donor support for capacity building remains unabated, their support for civil society is not. General budget support and the Poverty Reduction Strategy Paper (PRSP) processes illustrate the shift to state-centred development. Funds previously available for civil society are now being channelled through governments.

Donors are increasingly reticent about civil society, questioning CSO legitimacy and effectiveness. Some view CSOs as self-perpetuating, unelected, unaccountable and not necessarily either efficient or cost-effective. They are, they suggest, suffering from weak institutional capacity, management systems and dysfunctional organisational practices.

Many governments themselves do not have the capacity to engage effectively with civil society – even if they were committed to doing so. They do not always treat NGOs as serious partners, but engage instead in mere 'cosmetic' consultation. Consequently, in many places, government and civil society relations are characterised by mutual suspicion.

There is a fear that civil society is being pushed to the development periphery as mere sub-contractors to government. The increasing dependence of many NGOs, charities and non-profits on government contracts and commissions is a world-wide phenomenon. The increasing use of the term 'social enterprise' reflects this. Partnerships are therefore increasingly defined in contractual terms with all the associated power imbalances that exist between any contractor and service provider.

A second inter-related trend is towards greater donor harmonisation and alignment with national government priorities. This is outlined in the 2005 Paris Declaration on Aid Effectiveness. While ostensibly beneficial, civil society's role may be constricted in this new context because development initiatives are concentrated on recipient state priorities. It is questionable whether it is the role and priority of civil society simply to support government priorities. Many believe that civil society should be valued for its diversity and independence, not because it is an extension of the state.

What is the Paris Agenda?

In March 2005 the High Level Forum on Aid Harmonisation made the Paris Declaration. The EU, OECD, multilateral financing institutions, UN agencies and several non-OECD countries including Russia, India and China, signed a Statement of Resolve. The components are:

- Ownership: 'Partner countries exercise effective leadership over their development policies, and strategies and coordinate development actions'
- Alignment: 'Donors base their overall support on partner countries' national development strategies, institutions and procedures'
- Harmonisation: 'Donors implement common arrangements and simplify procedures'
- Managing for results: 'Managing resources and improving decision-making for results'
- Mutual accountability: 'Donors and partners are accountable for development results'.

The Paris Declaration accepts there are important 'remaining challenges': lack of institutional capacity in recipient countries; unpredictability of aid flows; insufficient delegation of authority in the field; mismatch between global initiatives and national development agendas and corruption. As a palliative, the Paris Agenda documents and the NGO Statement on Aid Harmonisation both stress the need for recipient government capacity building, The Paris Declaration commits recipient countries to integrate capacity building into their national development strategies.

(*source:* www.intrac.org/pages/aid_architecture.html)

It also raises an important anomaly: at the same time as promoting civil society's role in advocacy, alignment simultaneously reduces independent funding for civil society. If CSO funding is increasingly channelled through government, this will undermine their ability to be independent and hold government to account.

A third trend is that development funding is becoming more closely aligned with foreign policies. This may have always been the case; after all it was Richard Nixon who candidly commented 'Let us remember the main purpose of foreign aid is not to help other countries, but to help ourselves'. But geo-political changes have made this more stark. Recent appointments of career diplomats as heads of aid departments and aid departments being subsumed in Foreign Ministries illustrate this shift.

Post 9/11, the international aid objective to reduce poverty is being reframed into a more 'human security' agenda. As Alan Fowler notes: 'this political move is starting to send strong winds and tsunami-like undercurrents and waves through the aid system'. (2006:3)

We also have seen aid become increasingly militarised. A prime motive for any aid now is to serve the security agenda. Aid reconstruction is planned as part of the war effort. In Iraq and Afghanistan, for example, aid is increasingly linked to military interventions (Reality of Aid 2006). The 'war on terror' is being fought with aid as well as with armies.

How do Counter-Terrorism Measures (CTMs) affect Civil Society?

The worldwide ant-terrorism agenda has constricted support for civil society in three main ways:

1. by making financial reporting requirements more complex
2. by making international NGOs more risk-averse in partner selection
3. by providing authoritarian states with a tool that can be used to suppress critical civil society voices.

Tightened financial and administrative requirements raise the costs of compliance for CSOs. Smaller CSOs will find the requirements too burdensome, thereby concentrating funding in the hands of larger international CSOs

For international NGOs working with local civil society, there are risks of unintentional violation of CTMs. A small number of NGOs have been listed as 'Specially Designated Global Terrorists' due to perceived (but rarely explicit) links with terrorist groups.

In some cases, the aim is to bolster fragile governments, rather than strengthen an independent and autonomous civil society. For example, recent aid pledges to Pakistan are not primarily linked to development objectives but to Western security concerns. Furthermore, counter-terrorism measures are limiting the space for civil society by requiring strict controls over the movement of money. In some cases, this is undermining human rights, civil liberties and the right to protest about oppressive and unequal policies. This interventionist phase of international relations, based on the premise that 'we can control other countries with force', may translate into donors thinking that 'we can develop other countries with funds'.

A fourth trend is that donors have restored economic growth as a central plank in the development agenda – as it was in the 1960s and 1970s. Concerns about human development are once again being subsumed by an emphasis on indicators of economic growth. The area of social development, in which CSOs are most active, has been relegated in importance. The shift to contracting-out much aid work has meant that in many cases the primacy of the financial bottom-line takes precedence over development impact.

As well as private sector influences, capacity building has also been affected by the audit-orientation of public sector management that has permeated the aid world. There is an increasing pre-occupation in this new 'audit culture' with targets and other measures of efficiency (Hailey & Sorgenfrei, 2005). Because of the volatile and contradictory nature of the world, some suggest that many official donors, and public sectors generally 'feel a growing pressure to demonstrate its infallibility through logic, control and use of "objective" evidence for decision-making.' (Eyben, 2006:51)

Donors are increasingly driven by these measures of efficiency – disbursing large sums of money in a simple, cheap way and in as short a time as possible. This has contributed to a decentralisation of aid. It has also encouraged some donors to insist on funding CSOs through consortia, rather than individually. While making donor life easier, early studies (Ashman 2001, 2005) are far from conclusive about the benefits. In practice, consortia are extremely time-consuming for the CSOs involved and can result in the consortium only performing as well as the weakest member.

These shifts in donor aid are having strong ramifications, particularly influencing INGO behaviour. Many international NGOs are having to adjust their activities to align with these funding trends. This may contradict their greater understanding of capacity building outlined earlier. These factors have contributed to a more time-bound and contractual relationship between international NGOs and local partners. International NGOs tend to be more active and operational in implementing capacity building for partners themselves.

In an aid world that increasingly operates through service contracts, traditional notions of long-term 'partnerships' between Northern and Southern CSOs are giving way in many instances to short-term 'alliances', based on a specific time-bound contract. Many resource-scarce local CSOs feel they have little option but to accept their new status as mere implementers of international NGO projects.

The decentralisation of aid funding has also caused more international NGOs to open field offices; develop new federal or co federal structures; or to create new partner consortia or umbrella bodies to enable the distribution of funds. Such INGOs are thus placed in a better position to bid for large contracts. They tend to be more trusted by official donor agencies as they have capacity to manage and provide adequate accountability for large grants. Some of this is directly related to increased financial regulations imposed by counter-terrorism measures as well as tighter controls on risk management due to changes in charity law.

The pressure to be able to report positively on 'pre-set deliverables' puts pressure on international NGOs to be more controlling and 'micro-managing' of local CSOs. They need information systems to serve the accountability needs of the funding organisation, rather than the management needs of the local organisation.

In some cases, particularly in humanitarian relief and where there is limited local civil society capacity, INGOs are dispensing with the local partner altogether and becoming more operational themselves. A number of international NGOs who have previously operated exclusively through partners have now established their own operational emergency response team. This can set the international NGO in direct competition with local CSOs for both staff and financial resources, particularly as the emergency phase gives way to more developmental, rebuilding phases.

Conclusion

This brief overview has highlighted a number of perceived shifts in aid practice. While these may be more contested and complex than we are able to portray here, they do give a flavour of the contextual challenges facing civil society capacity building today – and tomorrow. To improve (and even maintain) the impact of our work, we need to have a strong appreciation of the potential implications of these trends.

PART 2

Principles of Good Practice in Capacity Building

In Part One we highlighted growing conceptual coherence about capacity building. Part Two will show a related consensus about what works in organisational capacity building – an emerging theory of good practice. Again, official agency reports, such as UNDP (2006) and DAC (2006) now concur with practitioner experience both from the South and the North. They mirror INTRAC's synthesis of practitioner experience (James and Wrigley 2007); the 2006 review of international NGO understanding of good practice (Lipson and Warren 2006); and internal analysis of INTRAC capacity building consultancies over the last eight years (Sorgenfrei 2004b; Beauclerk 2006 and 2007).

These conclusions resonate with what capacity builders have been saying for many years (CDRA in its annual reports since 1992, PRIA 1998, James 1994, 2001). Many of these conclusions were reinforced in the discussions at the 2006 INTRAC Capacity Building Conference. When the participants (a mixture of official donors, international NGOs, local capacity building providers and local CSOs from 49 countries) analysed their own experience of capacity building they prioritised the following 'enabling factors':

INTRAC Capacity Building Conference – The enabling factors

- treating capacity building as an endogenous process – ensuring that CSOs are in charge of their own capacity building processes
- transparently articulating actual stakeholder values, agendas, ethics and principles that underpin the capacity building
- challenging existing power dynamics through safe, yet open dialogue
- identifying how the human dimension affects capacity building. Personal characteristics of courage, curiosity, self-confidence, a sense of self-worth, self-esteem and dignity are essential amongst stakeholders.
- self-reflection and assessment
- emphasising building of trust and positive relationships between actors
- networking, rather than rivalry and competition
- working explicitly with gender and diversity issues are intrinsic to good capacity building
- having flexible, accessible and predictable funding, ideally controlled by civil society actors
- clarity in purpose, objectives, concepts, methodologies of capacity building
- situational and contextual relevance – ensuring that the process is adapted to the societal and organisational context.

There appears to be a degree of consistency as to what works and why. Although much of the evidence is drawn from the experience of organisational capacity building, we believe that these general principles hold true at whatever level of intervention (James 2005, Hailey 2006). However, we also recognise that these seemingly 'universal' human principles must be adapted to fit the specific context or cultural setting. Despite this proviso there appears to be a generally applicable theory of good practice. The central elements of this are described in the following three chapters.

Chapter 3 describes a **human, client-centred approach** that
- is people-centred and engages with values
- ensures client responsibility for change
- addresses issues of power and relationship.

Chapter 4 highlights a **locally appropriate and sustainable delivery process** that
- involves a variety of techniques
- explicitly adapts to the particular context and culture
- uses and develops skilled local capacity building providers.

Chapter 5 analyses good practice in **planning and management**
- pursues a carefully planned and 'situational' strategy
- focuses on implementation of the change process
- has developmental resourcing
- systematically assesses and learns from experience.

CHAPTER 3

A Human, Client-Centred Approach

'Development is about people. The rest is technique'.
Quoted by Bill Jackson, INTRAC 2006 Capacity Building Conference

If we look back on our own lives we know that change is a complex, dynamic process. It is emotional: at times exhilarating, at others frightening. But when we approach capacity building, we often forget the human dimension. We treat organisations as lifeless objects – logical machines, not living systems. The jargon we use implies capacity can be built from outside, as easily as a house. To make a difference, we need to put 'life' – a human dimension to change – into our capacity building. Specifically this means following the 'first principles' of development:

- being people-centred and engaging with values
- ensuring 'client' responsibility for change
- addressing issues of power and relationship.

People-Centred and Engaging with Values

It is almost a truism that organisations are composed of people. We know that leaders are human beings, not a collection of traits. Staff are more than just human resources. How any organisation behaves ultimately depends on how the people in it behave. Organisational capacity building is therefore a process of human change. Capacity building, however, is not just about separate individuals or organisations. It is a collective process about changing how individuals relate to each other. Thus good practice capacity building takes a people-centred approach that:

- Views people **holistically**. Individual and organisational behaviour is influenced by rational thinking and intellect, but also by emotion and even faith. Good capacity building practice consciously engages peoples' **emotions**. This is well-illustrated by 'Robbed of Dorothy' (Mboizi 2005) which is a moving story of an organisation's experience of HIV/AIDS. It was only when the organisation's leader was personally affected by the death of a close friend that he started to push the organisation to respond to HIV proactively. Clearly most resistance to change comes from our own

35

emotions. Fear and pride often need to be addressed. Some would also argue that capacity building is a holistic process that not just addresses such emotions but also incorporates a **spiritual** dimension (Senge et al 2004, Adair 2002, Handy 1991, James 2004). They believe that spiritual faith can have an important influence on behaviour. If an individual or organisation is to change the way they behave, the ability to draw on their personal faith (which underpins their values and assists in overcoming fears) is an important component.

- Places **values at the core of change**. People and organisations often change when there is a gap between their core values and their behaviour. A desire to align their behaviour with their values is what drives change. Research on leadership change in East Africa pointed out that: 'Values were the most important lever for change. The realisation that there was a considerable difference between the people they wanted to be (their core values) and the people they were (their leadership behaviour) was what drove the change process'. (James et al. 2005:29)

- Sees **self-awareness** as a critical first step in change. We do not change unless we realise where we are. Self-awareness through reflection for both individuals and organisations is essential in promoting change. It can vary from a formal organisational assessment procedure, to more informal notions of 'taking stock'; to facilitated discussions of 'where are we?' to intensely personal reflections, involving taking a 'fearless moral inventory'.

- Takes **gender** into consideration in any change process. The way people behave and change in organisations is influenced by their gender. For example, power, decision-making, relationships and even remuneration often have a gender dimension. Gender must be integrated into all capacity building work, rather than treated as a discrete topic. A human-centred approach to capacity building explicitly analyses the gender dimension.

- Engenders **hope and trust**. Capacity building has to bring hope and inspire people to change, to overcome their inherent human fear. Capacity building will not occur without hope and trust. This takes a more 'appreciative' rather than problem-centred approach to change. One technique that encapsulates the thinking behind is 'Appreciative Inquiry'. The text box below briefly describes this.

Appreciative Inquiry

Appreciative inquiry is a positive approach to change. It assumes that if you ask people about their problems you emphasise the problem. If you ask them about what works, they can learn how to replicate and develop positive behaviour. It is a cooperative search for the best in people, their organisation and the world around them. It asks questions such as:

- Describe a high-point experience in your organisation – a time when you felt most alive and engaged.
- What is it that you most value in yourself, your work and your organisation?
- What are the core factors that give life to your organisation?
- What three wishes do you have to enhance the health and vitality of your organisation?

Datta describes the effective use of an appreciative approach to change in Praxis Paper 28 (2007). He shows how such an approach allowed less tangible issues and concerns to be surfaced, such as hope, trust, unity, identity, and ownership. It enabled members to acknowledge and appreciate each others' abilities, thus helping to generate increased self-esteem and sense of ownership within their organisation.

The Vision Quest programme of leadership development (described in James 2005c) provides a good illustration of what a people-centred approach to capacity building looks like:

The Vision Quest Experience

The help offered to local NGO leaders by the South African-based Vision Quest exemplifies many of the best attributes of a personalised and process-based leadership development programme geared to changing attitudes and developing new solutions to old problems. The programme emphasises the leader as a human being, and what s/he wants to be. The Vision Quest approach is rooted in the belief that change has to start from within and leaders can only change their organisation if they can change themselves. It is designed to help participants think through their values and vision and develop a clear sense of their own identity.

Vision Quest strongly believes that behavioural change only really takes place when the learning experience is both intellectual and emotional. The programme not only creates time and space for busy leaders to reflect, but also urges them to challenge themselves. The belief is that the more that leaders become aware of their strengths and weaknesses and can develop strategies to work with them then the more effective they will be. To achieve this Vision Quest use a variety of learning methodologies including:

- triads: (small groups of three people discussing set questions or specific problems)
- journaling: (individual reflections and plans are written in personal journals)
- stories: (using narratives to illustrate issues or theories)
- mentoring pairs: (two pairs of two participants discuss personal issues, reflections and plans)
- physical exercise: (daily sessions to help unwind and relieve stress.)

As with many of the more respected leadership programmes, they take a holistic approach to the individual, and so look at different elements of the personal state – the socio-emotional, the physical, the spiritual and the mental and the linkages between them. But fundamental to the success of this programme is that it elicits hope, and helps individuals to identify the core purpose of their life. This is referred to as their quest. This process helps them generate a clearer sense of their own identity, which in turn enables them to balance external demands without compromising their core values.

Ensuring 'client' responsibility for change

Capacity building is about facilitating change – change to the dynamics or character of a particular organisation or the way they work, what they do and how they do it. Just as people only change when they take responsibility in a situation, so too with groups, communities, organisations and societies.

The prime factor in any capacity building is to ensure that the 'client' (the 'subject' of the capacity building intervention) is taking responsibility for the change process. They need to have internalised the need for change and be committed to following it through. So the first step in any capacity building work is to establish who wants to change and how much they want it. It is vital to locate the energy for change. Before starting it is important to ensure that the capacity building really is an internally-driven process. One of the key elements in the emerging consensus on the concept of capacity building from Chapter 1 is that it comes from within – an endogenous process. The motive for change must therefore be in the client.

Sometimes this is the case. Local CSOs develop their own capacity building programmes that address their own felt needs. They undertake their own participatory organisational assessment and develop their own objectives and indicators. The example from BRAC in Bangladesh, one of the largest NGOs in the world, illustrates this commitment:

BRAC's Own Capacity Building Initiatives

One of the key characteristics of a 'learning NGO' such as BRAC has been its willingness to invest in a continual process of learning and experimentation. It has encouraged innovation and been willing to learn from, and replicate, the work of other agencies and external specialists. BRAC has made considerable investments in its own research departments and training facilities. BRAC's preoccupation with staff development and training has been central to the way it operates. Indeed, training is largely seen as a strategic instrument to facilitate programme development. In the 1990s BRAC set aside seven per cent of its total salary budget for staff development alone. This is a remarkable figure when one considers that at the time it employed over 20,000 full-time employees and many more part-time.

Proactive investment in building capacity through training, research and internal learning enable NGOs like BRAC to grow and thrive. Such NGOs work hard at promoting and disseminating organisational learning. They see the benefits in the way they cope with external challenges, use resources more productively and, above all, in the way they help the communities with whom they work. The process of engaging staff in remembering, reflecting and learning is seen as a worthwhile investment and an essential component of organisation development and NGO capacity building.

But in reality the driver for change frequently comes from outside. All too often capacity building is at the behest of an outsider, often the donor. Donors see capacity building needs in their partners, more than themselves (a common human trait in most relationships!). Capacity building is something that 'we do for them'. The local organisation may not really feel the need for change. They acquiesce to donor suggestions for capacity building to secure funding, but do not necessarily have the commitment to capacity building to implement any change. Yet unless the individual, organisation or even society 'internalises' this need to change, there is no authentic motive for change and experience tells us that no significant change will occur.

Given that there are different purposes and interests in capacity building, the critical question is: whose agenda predominates? It is therefore important for stakeholders to openly articulate their interests in capacity building to reach agreement about 'shared agendas' – but in such a way as the client still retains responsibility for change. Given the perceived power imbalances in such discussions, this is no easy feat. Local NGOs may feel that donor control over resources gives them little option but to acquiesce.

The following example from Sri Lanka is an excellent example of how ownership of the capacity building process shifted before the planned start of a programme.

Wresting Ownership from the Donor

Three donor agencies working in Sri Lanka were experiencing common problems with their partners and contracted an international consultant to undertake a Training Needs Analysis. The questionnaires told them what they expected to hear and they designed a training programme focussing on Planning, Monitoring and Evaluation. The donors selected a handful of local personalities as a Steering Committee to oversee the process,

The committee agreed with the donor goals, but were so concerned about the process that they decided to conduct their own assessment. Although they used similar questions, they received starkly different responses. Local partners opened up and shared their real fears and uncertainties in working in such a volatile and turbulent context. As a result, the steering committee came up with a very different way forward for capacity building.

The donors expressed strong reservations about the steering committee's proposal. They felt it would not be 'proper technical training' and might exacerbate local divisions. A long 'tug-of-war' ensued, before the donors reluctantly agreed to abandon their plans and follow the suggestions of the locally-led process.

It is so important for the client to take responsibility for the change process because effective capacity building is an endogenous process. As Eyben points out in the aid world: 'There has been little public discussion of what we have learnt from psychology: that ultimately the only people we can change are ourselves and that in order to be part of the solution, donors must recognise they are part of the problem.' (2006:2).

Capacity building is not simply about learning new skills and acquiring new knowledge. It is also about giving up bad habits and behaving in new ways. It can involve admitting error or ignorance. Change is often a painful and difficult process. It is usually sensitive and personal. We have to really want it if we are to overcome the natural desire to remain in the comfort zone we are in. The motive for change must be stronger than the incentives to remain the same. Not surprisingly there is some ambivalence towards capacity building. We want it, but at the same time we do not want to change.

Good practice capacity articulates and interrogates the agendas for change at the outset:

- Who knows about the problem?
- Who can solve the problem?

- Who is taking responsibility for the problem?
- Who within the organisation is motivated to change?
- Who needs to be motivated to change?

Individual leaders need to take responsibility for change in their own organisations. Visionary leaders often play a key role in inspiring or even forcing people out of the comfort of the familiar. This requires individual courage, will and determination. But it is much more than that. There must be a collective motive to change and sense of responsibility. A critical mass of dissatisfaction with the status quo can develop into a collective motive for change. This collective motive for is change is assisted when people feel they have had the opportunity to contribute meaningfully to the identification of both the needs to change as well as the appropriate ways forward.

The sense of responsibility for change is not static. It can be lost or gained over time. The means the methods of capacity building must retain and even develop 'client' ownership and responsibility of the change process. Consequently good practice capacity building involves the staff of the organisation. For example, in responding to the capacity building demands of working in a context of high HIV prevalence, you must involve all staff in the process of policy development – otherwise there will be no buy-in, no shift in the culture of silence and stigma and consequently no change (Hadjipateras et al. 2006).

Means, Motive and Opportunity

INTRAC Praxis has investigated the practice of capacity building over the last four years (James and Wrigley 2007). We have learnt that there needs to be *motive*, *means* and *opportunity* (taking a metaphor from detective investigation as Britton 2005 suggested).

A strong internal *motive* for change is critical. Individuals, organisations and societies will not change for the better without a good reason. We need to find out who has the motive for change.

The *means* and methods of good practice in capacity building are becoming clear. They include methods that retain and develop ownership; are people-centred and relational; engage with peoples' values and emotions; use a variety of approaches and adapt to context and culture.

The *opportunity* to change is just as important, yet frequently missed. Our busyness suffocates the opportunity to implement change. We may assume that once a capacity building 'event' has taken place capacity has been built. But we all know from New Year's resolutions that planning to change and actually changing are not the same thing!

Experience shows that we have done well in focusing on good practice means and methods, but have failed to adequately consider the importance of motive and opportunity.

All those affected by any capacity building process need to have real and valued incentives to encourage their involvement in the process. Such incentives can be tangible (e.g. financial, promotion) or intangible (e.g. improved morale, better team dynamics), but, in any case, they need to be provided in a timely and appropriate manner.

Addressing issues of relationships and power

Capacity building is about shifts in relationships. It is not just about one individual or even one organisation. Capacity building issues permeate relationships throughout the aid system – within communities; between the community and the CSO; within the CSO; between the CSO and the international NGO; between the INGO and the government aid department; between the government aid department and other ministries and Parliament – the list could go on. This approach builds on systems thinking in which the inter-connectivity of all the elements is a defining characteristic.

Good practice capacity building therefore takes a more open-systems perspective – not compartmentalising problems in one element. Instead of taking a discrete approach to change, it takes a more systemic approach. This is why authentic capacity building is not something that we can do for others. It is a two-way process at least. Capacity building has to influence our relationships with others and therefore has to influence us.

Each of these relationships is infused with its own power dynamics. Capacity building which shifts relationships is therefore not a-political. As Morgan points out: 'It is not power neutral. Where capacities are built there are both winners and losers. Capacity-building cannot be disconnected from issues of power, competition for resources or control over them' (1996:15).

The importance of the personal and relational is well-illustrated by the review of CABUNGO, a Malawian capacity building provider (Wrigley 2006). The most significant changes that clients of CABUNGO identified as a result of capacity building interventions were about personal change as well as shifts in power and relationship:

Personal and Relational Change through Capacity Building

Clients said CABUNGO helped them:

- become more self-aware at individual and organisational levels
- shift relationship between leadership, staff and board thus creating more ownership, motivation, energy, passion and empowerment
- adapt organisational actions in new, self-defined ways
- become more organised by 'putting the house in order' – i.e. structures, systems, competencies and funding
- have more trust internally
- change the way the organisation relates to others, e.g. the communities in which they work and the donors that fund them.

Capacity building therefore involves positive shifts in power and relationships within and between organisations. Good practice methods therefore address relationships. Leadership development for example, is not just about developing an individual, but developing the relationships between leaders and followers. It also recognises the potentially creative or destructive tensions in human relationships. Good quality capacity building strengthens relational skills to enable people to manage conflict creatively, rather than ignore conflict or even fuel it.

Good practice capacity building explicitly challenges existing dysfunctional power dynamics within groups, organisations and between different actors. The IFCB report on capacity building concluded that:

> 'It is easy for donors, seen by recipients as very powerful in their ability to control essential resources, to remain unaware of how much communications can be distorted by real or perceived power asymmetries. Potential beneficiaries of capacity building programmes may be reluctant to explain what kinds of programmes are really needed for fear they will be seen as unworthy of future support... If capacity building initiatives embody or reinforce Northern dominance and Southern dependence, then programme impacts are likely to be counter productive'.
> (quoted in James 2001:138).

Conclusion

Capacity building is first and foremost a human process. Capacity building will not occur unless people can change. We must avoid the temptation to reduce and over-simplify capacity building into a lifeless technical process. Organisations are not machines, but collections of complex human beings. We need to handle them with care.

CHAPTER 4

Locally Appropriate and Sustainable Provision of Capacity Building

We have seen how important it is to take a human-centred approach to capacity building. But the ways in which organisational capacity building services are delivered also has an impact on the effectiveness of an intervention or programme. The method and vehicle for delivery of capacity building is important. In Chapter 4 we identify three crucial elements of good practice:

- use of a variety of methods
- explicit adaptation to the particular context and culture
- use and development of skilled local capacity building providers

Using a variety of methods

Capacity building relies on a wide variety of tools and methods. Experience tells us that variation is necessary because organisations are made up of diverse people, who learn in different ways and from different methods. These different methods can mutually reinforce each other. A mixture of methods therefore is more likely to promote change. This is illustrated in the example from Macedonia below:

MCIC Methods in Macedonia

To build capacity of CSOs in Macedonia, MCIC uses a mixture of methods:

- consultancy
- open training
- in-house training
- study visits
- secondments
- on-the-job training
- peer counselling
- mentoring and coaching

(*source Beauclerk 2007*)

In the past training has been the preferred mode of capacity building. Looking at capacity building in the Balkans, Sterland referred to CSOs being 'trained to death' (2006). Training is easier and simpler to plan and fund than more informal and evolutionary processes. Training can easily avoid the messier, more complex and unpredictable nature of capacity building. It may prevent getting embroiled in the personal – yet it is the personal values and beliefs that determine behaviour. While training is still a very important capacity building method, it should not be the only one.

Some of the recent trends and innovations in capacity building methods suggest a shift towards:

- periodic, rather than one-off, inputs
- working with specific individuals (often leaders) and developing teams while bearing in mind the whole organisation's development
- appreciating the influence of history and the need to consider the future when making changes
- accepting the need to work on both 'hard' and 'soft' issues.

Although training still appears to be the prime methodology used, it appears to be becoming more modular. A number of examples of good practice from capacity building practitioners describe capacity building processes with a number of short training inputs over a period of 4–18 months (James and Wrigley 2007). This space between inputs allows participants to digest, apply and implement the learning from the training inputs. It also provides the opportunity for support from mentors or peers between modules.

Coaching and mentoring are also an example of the emphasis on personal change in specific individuals, particularly leaders, within the context of a wider organisational change process. The INTRAC review of mentoring and coaching colourfully describe them as being: 'on the "A" list of capacity building celebrities today. It seems you cannot read a review of good practice capacity building without coming across mentoring and coaching. Any self-respecting leadership development has coaching and mentoring present'. (Deans et al. 2006:1). Coaching and mentoring are seen as particularly useful methods for working with senior mangers who have reached a certain stage in their career (when attending formal training courses has less impact) and in helping to develop female leaders, because they can develop confidence and self-belief.

Experiential and process-led approaches are critically important to good practice in promoting individual change and group development. These rely on learning through doing and often entail a range of exercises, simulations or case studies. They are marked by their innovative nature, and often try to address highly personal issues. For example, the exercise from Cambodia, described below, illustrates how a creative, but culturally appropriate, process can surface and address deep-seated fears that determine behaviour. This exercise is a good example of how a workshop can be made experiential, personal, and gender conscious for a specific cultural context.

> **Destroying the minefield of fear**
>
> Fear is one of the most powerful and controlling factors in women's lives in Cambodia but they are rarely articulated. To make women's fears more explicit and therefore easier to deal with, we created an exercise using the very familiar danger of landmines.
>
> In the first step the group sat in a circle and answered questions that all started with 'What frightens you about …' and ended with a range of subjects such as men, other women, living in Phnom Penh, and so on. Each answer was both spoken and written on a card and put into the centre. Next we grouped the cards and wrote the headings of the different groups onto circles of paper of varying sizes, up to a meter in diameter. We laid these circles on the floor to create the group's fears' minefield. The range of subjects was wide and varied from concerns about men's domination of women, violence, second wives, health, money and even traffic issues. One participant spoke for others when she said: 'I live my life constantly in fear, but I never thought about it like this before. Breaking it down into pieces has given me clarity to see all the things that I am frightened about and understand that some are small and unimportant, while others are strong.'
>
> At the end of the workshop, we moved the experience to a physical level as each participant tried to tiptoe through the minefield without stepping on any of the fears. They found it a powerful manifestation of how they live their lives. Everyone then chose one fear that she felt she could and should get rid of. Physically destroying the chosen fear while sharing the why and or how they would deal with it in reality was an empowering and energising experience.
>
> *Source: Jenny Pearson, personal communication at 2006 INTRAC Conference*

This example also shows the impact of history on individual behaviour and the legacy of conflict on a local community. In a similar way, many organisational assessment or even future-oriented strategic processes emphasise the importance of understanding the history of the organisation. Time-lines are common exercises in many capacity building processes today.

We have also seen greater acceptance of the need to integrate both 'hard' and 'soft' approaches to capacity building. Earlier capacity building work tended to focus exclusively on management systems. Training was commonly given in financial systems, project management and reporting systems. This donor interest in the 'nuts and bolts' of accountability remains unabated. But now the emphasis on the 'harder' systems side of capacity building is complemented by work on the 'softer' people issues. For example, we know that when building capacity to mainstream HIV, changes are needed both at a system and individual level. Merely writing an HIV policy without addressing attitudes of stigma will not bring about change (Hadjipateras 2006), except on a cosmetic level. Or on a wider scale, the World Bank is seeking to reinforce its Good Governance agenda with support to matters of leadership ethics and integrity, through the Global Integrity Alliance. It is not a question of either systems or people, but 'both / and'.

Explicitly adapting methods to culture and context

Analysis of capacity-building interventions has clearly demonstrated 'the profound and far-reaching influence which the different contexts had'. (James 2001:124). The way people think, feel, behave and change is very strongly influenced by the culture and context in which they live. The development sector inherently involves situations where people work across cultures and contexts, e.g. between international and local partners or between urban and rural staff. The influences of culture and context can strongly affect and shape good quality capacity. These influences include: values and beliefs, attitudes and assumptions, sense of space and time, language and communication, habits and traditions, history, social hierarchies, gender, and faith.

Analysis of the Praxis Papers which looked at the perspectives on capacity building from France, Spain, Iran, Bosnia Herzegovina and Kosovo revealed how different meanings were attached to capacity building in each country (James and Wrigley 2007). Even amongst the donor states of the UK, USA, France and Spain there are significant differences: Anglophone capacity building is perceived as more about organisations and results, whereas Francophone capacity building is more about individuals and processes. Unless we understand intimately the context that we are operating from and operating into, we may well blunder in with foreign and superficial solutions that do not meet underlying needs.

The impact of context and culture can be likened to the influence of the soil and climate on a plant's growth. Different cultures and contexts will give rise to different capacity-building needs, and will require different approaches and skills to address those needs appropriately and effectively. Ignorance of such important external variables may result in inappropriate 'blueprint' approaches to capacity-building.

Good practice capacity building therefore starts with a thorough understanding of the context and how this might affect individual and organisational behaviour. It should respect local forms of knowledge; and explore what capacity building means in the particular culture. This analysis should influence the choice of capacity building methods. For example, using highly participatory methods may not be appropriate in cultures that are used to a very formal way of working. Rather than stimulating capacity building, they may create confusion and heighten people's resistance to new ideas and change.

Good capacity building practice involves culturally-sensitive communication. The language of capacity building brings with it all sorts of culturally and politically-loaded baggage, that makes it appear 'foreign', donor-driven and external. Clearly this is an anathema to the aim of client ownership. For example, something as seemingly innocuous as 'learning' may need adaptation as practitioners found in Cambodia. As the Khmer word that directly translates as 'learning' is confusing and potentially divisive, they had to use the local equivalent of 'wisdom' which was not (Pearson 2006).

In a similar way, Chiku Malunga advocates use of indigenous forms of communication – in his context, African proverbs (2004:1). He says:

'The failure of so many development interventions over the past half-century can be partly attributed to their lack of rootedness in the society they were designed to *change. For development interventions to catalyse fundamental change, they have to engage with people's identity and values, whether they be individuals, communities, organisations or indeed nations. Capacity building needs to be grafted onto pre-existing foundational values, not simply importing another's value base.'*

Using proverbs can help to connect with people's identity and values. In this case the traditional wisdom contained in African proverbs is applied both to understanding organisations and to improving their performance. This use of proverbs presents a new and creative way of communicating and discussing organisational principles that transcends the normal barriers to good communication. It therefore offers an important means to make capacity building more effective.

Another good way to adapt methods to culture and context is to use story-telling. Stories can connect capacity building with people's own lives. Illustration and cartoons are also useful in assisting people to reflect on capacity building issues and think in a creative way (Crooks 2004). Cartoons can clarify a situation in a memorable and amusing way that is accessible to all. Such a process enables people to think outside their customary logical, rational way, often releasing energy and reducing tensions (Hailey, James, Wrigley, 2005). In addition, locally appropriate metaphors and images can be used – such as adapting the traditional 'iceberg' analogy to the image of a hippo (to highlight the importance of the informal, invisible organisational dynamics that take place below the water-line).

Using and fostering local capacity building providers

Good practice capacity building often benefits from having external providers of facilitation, training, consultancy and coaching services. External capacity building providers often provide catalytic inputs into a process, provided they do so in a way that retains client ownership. This role can be critical in providing a structure and an external perspective to the process. They can bring learning from other organisations. They can inject energy and reduce tension and ensure the CSO does not get caught up and distracted by its own work. They can also provide monitoring and follow-through.

Capacity building providers are often contracted in as independent consultants to provide external expertise. They either operate on a freelance basis or are part of some sort of capacity building support agency (e.g. CDRA, INTRAC etc) which will charges for their services. The choice of capacity builder is crucial and needs to be researched. It is important to see such an intervention as an on-going investment and not a recurrent cost to be born grudgingly.

Good practice indicates that wherever possible local capacity building providers should be used. Provided they have the skills and attitudes required, local consultants should bring a better understanding and appreciation of the culture and context. They are on-hand for follow-up and they provide an on-going resource for the sector.

In many places, however, there is a dearth of good quality local capacity building providers for CSOs. This is why it is so important to use those that do exist and develop others. For example SNV, a Dutch NGO is changing its strategy to work with more local capacity building suppliers:

SNV working alongside local providers

In 2000, SNV changed its strategy. Moving away from project implementation for donors, it became an independent advisory organisation supporting capacity development of local actors. It hired more local staff to provide capacity building services. SNV has decided a major strategic shift will be to increasingly work with local capacity builders. This will involve sub-contracting local providers and involving them in SNV's own capacity building practice.

This does not mean that foreigners have nothing to offer. They can bring an external perspective that shares learning and experience from other countries and is not embroiled in some local constraints. Foreigners would do well to work alongside local consultants in a way that cross-fertilises their different skills and experiences.

The credibility, experience and expertise of those facilitating a capacity building process are crucial. The skill of the capacity builder is not just how best to apply different approaches or techniques, but is in gaining the trust and respect of the parties involved. Often they will have to handle the sensitive power dynamics without being seen to take sides. They have to work with any tensions and conflicts that arise. Consequently they need to be highly aware of their own position of power as well as the power dynamics at play in the situation.

Obviously different providers will bring different expertise and strengths. Some will focus on the tangible, the formal and the technical, while others will stress the intangible, the informal and the developmental. For some it is about filling gaps and correcting deficits while to others it is about empowerment and releasing latent capacity. To some it is about mobilising resources, building relationships and developing infrastructure, while to others it is a psychotherapeutic process intended to influence behaviour and change attitudes.

But whatever approach is adopted, experience suggests that much of their success depends on whether they are used in a timely and sensitive manner. Effective capacity builders adapt different approaches and methodologies. They balance the hard and the soft, the instrumental with the open-process. It is the ability to marry 'hard', systems skills with intangible, 'soft' skills or competencies. The real challenge for capacity builders is to know what will work when. This depends on insight and experience, analysis and intuition, sensitivity and strategic clarity.

James and Wrigley (2007) chart some of the characteristics of good quality capacity building providers:

Qualities of Good Capacity Builders

- develop client-ownership of the process to ensure the client takes responsibility for their change process. Good facilitators cultivate the 'will to change'
- take a people-centred approach to change, using exercises that encourage reflection, learning and personal growth: they need to be able to work with emotions and manage tensions creatively
- see the inter-relationships between elements and examine how: extended relations can affect leadership behaviour; staff relationships affect organisational behaviour; inter-organisational relationships can influence impact and global events may impact the organisation
- understand and challenge power dynamics in a sensitive and courageous way
- have the confidence and competence to use a variety of methods, including the more experiential
- balance structure and flexibility e.g. provide clear frameworks but allow emergence and adaptation happen
- engage in open and equal dialogue and communicate in a culturally sensitive and creative way
- recognise and respond sensitively to the influences of culture and context: they also need the agility to shift and adapt to a changing context, developing new competencies as they become necessary for the client.

(taken from James and Wrigley 2007)

These skills are based on more fundamental underlying attitudes. Participants at the 2006 INTRAC conference highlighted the importance of the following attitudes of good quality capacity building providers.

- belief in the existing and latent capacities of clients (not just being aware of their weaknesses)
- openness to hearing and understanding the client
- openness to hearing and understanding the client
- self-confidence to negotiate and not compromise on principles and values
- the humility to work with others and ask for external support themselves if necessary
- courage and determination to persevere.

We know from our own experience that we change as a result of what someone else has said or done. This is why the providers of capacity building services are such a critical ingredient in the change process. The demands on their skills, wisdom and emotional intelligence are extremely high. In many resource-poor contexts, there are not many capacity building providers who meet such demands and who chose to work with CSOs. This is why it is so important to use and develop local providers of capacity building services for CSOs.

We now move on to other key elements in taking a strategic approach to capacity building.

CHAPTER 5

Planning and Management of Capacity Building

'Almost everything about building capacity in non-profits takes longer and is more complicated than one would expect. Building capacity can feel like a never ending process because improvements in one area of practice have a way of placing unexpected new demands on other areas'
(McKinsey 2001).

Capacity building does not occur by chance. To be effective, it needs good planning and management. Experience has shown us that this involves:

- adopting a carefully planned and contextualised strategy (adjusted to the national, regional and organisational context)
- concentrating on the implementation of the change process
- resourcing the process with adequate 'hands-off' financing
- continually assessing and learning from experience.

Pursuing a carefully planned and contextualised strategy

A good capacity building plan starts with a thorough analysis of the context and culture and examines how they affect the proposed capacity building needs and solutions. This plan will be more like an indicative road map that evolves over time. Milestones and monitoring are therefore vital to adapt the capacity building process to the reality experienced.

Capacity building needs to adapt to both the local culture and the particular organisational context. Different types of organisation face particular capacity building challenges and will respond differently. We will illustrate some of the differences when working with community based organisations (CBOs), faith-based organisations (FBOs) and civil society networks.

We know capacity building is a complex process of human change. We have to take capacity building seriously to make a difference. Capacity is not built by accident. We have learnt that for capacity building to work, we need to take a coherent, systematic approach.

At the outset, a well-planned approach involves different stakeholders developing a shared clarity around the concept, purpose, objectives and methodologies for a capacity-building initiative. This needs to happen within agencies and between agencies. We have learnt the value of making time at the start of the process to explore the different, and not always complementary, agendas and interests involved. This allows us to negotiate and identify common ground.

Careful planning should not bring rigidity. Quality capacity building needs to have the flexibility to respond to 'where the energy for change is', rather than relentlessly pursue artificial targets dreamt up for the proposal some years earlier. A carefully planned strategy towards capacity building also recognises that capacity already exists. It values and builds on past experiences and existing capacities to form a solid basis to establish the parameters for the work.

We know that capacity building needs and solutions are powerfully influenced by both the culture and the context. For example, throughout sub-Saharan Africa the onslaught of HIV/AIDS is decimating capacity, forcing organisations to address new and complex needs. This includes human resource procedures, staff planning policies, strategy development, financial resource needs and internal relations issues. In such contexts, the whole goal of capacity building may shift towards simply capacity maintenance (James 2004).

Capacity building processes need to evolve to fit the changing circumstances. Sterland, for example, identified six distinct phases of capacity building as the Balkans moved from an immediate post-conflict crisis to minimum security, then to a state of flux and trauma prior to increasing political stability and, finally, a return of displaced people and a functioning local municipal government (2006).

Capacity building also needs to be 'contextualised' with respect to the type of organisation. We examine the particular distinctiveness of capacity building needs and approaches with three popular types of CSO: CBOs, FBOs and networks. Obviously other types of CSOs will have their own distinctive capacity building features and approaches.

CBOs are grassroots organisations set up by those belonging to a specific geographical community. The size of their operations is relatively small scale, they work in a particular community; they are membership-based and rarely legally registered. These CBOs may include, for example, groups of women's, farmers, youth, pastoralists, forest users and other kinds of self-help groups. Past attempts to build their capacity have often treated CBOs as the same as more formal NGOs. In the text box below Wright-Revolledo highlights some of the critical situational differences in capacity building with CBOs:

What is different about capacity building with CBOs?

- The members of CBOs may be inter-related and beholden to leaders outside the CBOs. As a result it is vital to be particularly sensitive to understanding community power relationships, local kinship structures and intra-household dynamics
- CBOs can be fluid. They may disappear and remerge in different and unpredictable ways. It may be the internalisation of skills (individual 'residual capacity') that is more important than the sustainability of the CBOs itself
- It is important to understand what brings people together in particular communities and how this changes over time and in response to political, socio-economic and cultural change
- Members of CBOs can, but do not necessarily, represent the interests of those external to it. It is important to understand how the benefits of capacity building might extend to or exclude others, including the ultra poor
- The organisational culture of CBOs is likely to reflect power differentials and gender imbalances that exist in the community at large. Such an understanding needs to be built into capacity building
- As volunteer CBO 'staff' may have lower literacy levels and greater time constraints than formal NGO staff capacity building may thus take longer.

(Adapted from Wright-Revolledo 2006)

Capacity building with faith-based organisations (FBOs) is also different from capacity building with secular NGOs. INTRAC's experience with FBOs shows us a number of distinctive features that we need to appreciate.

What is different about capacity building with FBOs?

The particular organisational features of FBOs that INTRAC looks at are:
- The relationships between the development organisation (or programme/department) and the religious structure – both in formal governance and informal relationships
- How the beliefs influence the development strategy. Does it affect why and how they work? Does it affect who they work with and for what ends?
- How the perceived dimension of 'spiritual authority' affects leadership and cultural norms
- How the faith affects staffing in terms of motivation, recruitment, line management and behaviour.

INTRAC's experience suggests capacity building works better when it:
- understands the FBO as being an integral part of a wider religious institution and the implications for its identity, governance and relationships
- includes the wider religious institution within the FBO change process
- addresses common FBO organisational issues of strategy, leadership, culture and management systems
- explores the meaning of what its faith-base means to the FBO client and the implications this has for its approach to development and its staffing
- integrates any capacity building process with the faith of the client.

In the last decade, networks of CSOs have become the favoured actors in development for two main reasons. First, donors have emphasised the importance of civil society's 'voice' in policy formulation and governance and seen CSO networks as the most obvious and effective expression of it. Secondly, they are also seen as a convenient vehicle for channelling donor funds to their members.

However, networks are extremely complex organisational forms to manage effectively. Different stakeholders ask them to play a multiplicity of potentially conflicting roles. To be effective networks need both a strong membership base and a strong coordinating secretariat. They are far from being the convenient and simple solution sought by many development planners. Networks of CSOs are extremely complex organisational forms to manage well. They are not the same as 'normal' NGOs. They face inherent strategic paradoxes that raise particular capacity challenges. These include:

Common capacity challenges of networks

- **Identity**: As networks develop, members often create a secretariat to serve them better. Over time, secretariats do more and more on behalf of the members, taking over control. Members disengage.

- **Leadership** structure and decision-making: networks need to be both representative of members' views, but also able to respond flexibly and rapidly to immediate issues.

- **Strategy**: Networks are often torn by competing demands of their members and cannot undertake all the potential roles wanted by members - advocacy, capacity building, co-ordination and/or funding.

- **Resourcing**: Do the members fund the network or do they solicit outside funding? In practice, CSO networks often get donor funding which undermines members' ownership and creates a 'donor project' orientation.

This highlights some of the differences in building capacity of different types of organisation. But even within these categories, each individual organisation is also unique. Each faces its own distinctive challenges. Effective capacity building adapts to the needs of different organisations in different situations.

Focusing on the Implementation of Change

Good practice capacity building focuses on the implementation of change, not just the planning of it. We can sometimes sub-consciously assume that once a capacity building 'event' has taken place, capacity has been built. We inadvertently equate a capacity building or strategic plan with its actual implementation. We think we have a new strategy just because we have a new plan.

We all have experience of participants returning inspired from training, but either the weight of work, or the lack of opportunity or authority inhibits any change. We know organisations that have planned to change their strategy and drop certain activities, only to get overtaken by the need to secure funding to pay salaries. Also our hectic individual and organisational schedules preclude capacity building. We expect quick immediate results preferably with numerical proof of impact. But implementing change needs time and sensitive management.

Experience and practice suggests that indicative plans need be drawn up to provide a road map and facilitate scheduling of activities. Progress needs to be monitored and staff need be kept fully informed of developments. Resources need to be allocated to facilitate the implementation stage, and those charged with implementing the change process must be supported and supervised.

The success of any capacity building initiative depends on proactive leadership. There needs to be an individual or team to 'champion' the process. But such leadership is not just about encouraging good practice or promoting a vision. It is as much about steering the process of capacity building through its many iterations and helping all involved to grow, develop and cope with the consequences of the change process in which they are engaged.

The implementation of change also needs resourcing. Good practice capacity building purposefully resources and manages implementation. There are always time costs and often a financial cost too. Sadly, with capacity building, it is often only the planning of the job that gets funded. Capacity building events, such as strategic planning sessions, HIV policy development processes and training courses, are what get funded. Better organised ones end up with action plans. But then the capacity building funding stops. There is often nothing planned or provided for the change process itself. But the real work of change, which only takes place back in the organisation, has not yet begun.

To ensure there is sufficient opportunity to implement change capacity building interventions need to take more of a process perspective, allow sufficient time, ensure follow-up to implementation is built in from the start and provide for longer time-frames.

Hands-off 'Developmental' Resourcing

Donors can play a number of useful roles in making capacity building work. They can put capacity building issues onto another organisation's agenda. For example, one Ugandan capacity building provider (CDRN) describes how: 'One of our main donors, CORDAID, had entered into a long-term relationship with us and one of the key objectives was about helping partners with HIV/AIDS and health issues'. (Mboizi 2005)

Donors can also provide information and contacts to partners, putting them into contact with others from whom they can learn, documenting and disseminating learning and enabling exposure visits. But the key role, if not the most attractive one, is that of funding the capacity building process.

Implementing good practice capacity building is expensive and time-consuming. It requires enlightened donors support, who see capacity building as a longer-term investment, rather than an annual expense. Such donors have to treat capacity building as a process that includes the implementation of change, rather than discrete one-off training events. These enlightened donors are prepared to subordinate their own agendas to those of their partners.

However, for many donors these are considerable challenges. Aid trends encourage donors to disburse large amounts of money quickly, with risk minimised in order to generate visible and reportable results for their own back donors. Their interests may be very different from those of local CSO partners (though there may obviously be some overlap). If donors accept that capacity building is endogenous, and will therefore only be effective if the local partner's agenda is paramount, then they must relinquish control of the capacity building targets as well as the time-frame – even though this does not fit easily with the prevailing demands of the aid system for immediate and measurable results.

One example of enlightened and situational donor support is the work of four Dutch NGOs through StopAidsNow! (SAN!). They realised that the capacity of partners in countries with a high HIV/AIDS prevalence was having a considerable impact on the capacity of their partners. They developed a major capacity building initiative to strengthen 80 local partners, initially in Uganda and India. As well as funding the capacity building inputs over an extended period, these donors have undertaken to adapt their funding procedures to reinforce the capacity building aims. For example, they do not just support partners to develop HIV policies, but they also commit themselves to supporting their implementation. These donors have collaboratively developed their own guidelines for funding that they call 'Good donorship in a time of HIV/AIDS'. The text box below highlights some of the core principles of their funding approach:

SAN! Good Donorship Principles Around HIV/AIDS

- All donors should fund a share of their partners' overheads, including the cost of workplace policies, in addition to funding projects or activities.

- The impacts of HIV/AIDS can cause partners to produce lower levels of outputs for the same investment.

- The cost of inaction is greater than the cost of action to manage the impacts of HIV/AIDS.

- Partners are responsible for implementing, monitoring and evaluating their own workplace policies. However, we will support them as set out in the commitments contained in these guidelines.

- Donors and partners need to communicate openly about the challenges brought about by HIV/AIDS and are committed to doing so.

- Partners need to create workplace policies to fit their context, if they are to have effective policies they can sustain. Partners must decide who to include in their workplace policies. We expect that their policies will attend to gender issues.

Assessing Impact and Learning from Experience

Good practice capacity building involves taking a systematic approach to monitoring and evaluation (M&E). We need this information for decision-making, learning, and accountability. As Cracknell warns: 'Unless some evidence of attributable impact of capacity-building programmes is presented, donor support for capacity-building will be severely reduced'.

(2000:263). We need to reflect on and learn from our experiences in order to change and improve our capacity building work in the future.

At the 2006 INTRAC Capacity Building conference, participants reflected on their own experiences of capacity building and identified common 'footprints of change'. These are outlined in the text box below:

Footprints of Change at INTRAC Capacity Building Workshop 2006

 Workshop participants highlighted changes at different levels.

The Capacity building process: Many of the perceived footprints of change were in fact descriptions of the capacity building process. Participants spoke of methods such as technical assistance, facilitation, dialogue, exchanges and information. They also highlighted good practice in capacity building such as using culturally appropriate methods embedded in the context, taking appropriate time to achieve results and, addressing power issues and being flexible.

Organisational changes: Examples of footprints of change at this level included: increased conceptual understanding, vision and improved self-esteem. Further indicators included abilities to manage growth, be resilient and adaptable, maintain IT systems and fund-raise locally.

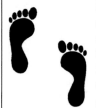 **Beneficiary level changes:** The impact on advocacy issues such as debt and landmines were given as examples of success on a global scale. National level impacts included civil society voices influencing policy formulation – including having input into Poverty Reduction Strategy Papers (PRSPs). Capacity building has contributed to improved access to basic services in communities. In some cases there has been greater community ownership of processes and greater confidence and power.

Measuring changes in organisational capacity is certainly not an easy task. Difficult questions immediately leap to mind:

- What changes are we measuring? As we have seen, capacity building is beset by definitional problems.
- How can we be sure that the change is the result of the capacity building? There are inherent challenges of attribution.
- What would have happened if there had been no capacity building? There are also challenges of never knowing for sure what would have happened without the input – the counter-factual.
- Whose perspective are we evaluating from? What looks like success to the donor may be perceived as failure locally and vice versa. Whose measures count?
- When do we evaluate impact – after ten weeks, ten months or ten years?
- How do we get meaningful numbers? Most aid decisions require some sort of quantification – results are increasingly seen in quantitative terms.
- How do we convert complex and lengthy data to useable knowledge? For example Sida have to distil meaning from the 10,000 pages of M&E reports they receive each year (quoted at 2006 conference).

In M&E of capacity building the 'best' is easily the enemy of the 'good'. Frequently extremely time-consuming and expensive M&E processes are designed, but never implemented. Clearly there are major issues of attribution and measuring intangible changes in relationships, but these can be partially mitigated. It is better to undertake a more limited and qualified evaluation, rather than none at all. Even basic impact assessment can add real value to the capacity building process.

There is often a difference of opinion as to whether capacity building impact can be quantified or whether it should remain qualitative. There are certainly ways of generating numbers and percentage improvements (as the example from Guyana quoted in the Introduction demonstrated). There are even ways of doing a very simple cost-benefit analysis (James 2004). But because capacity building is a complex human process, any numbers will require considerable qualification. They could be so artificial as to be meaningless. Taylor warns that 'to capture the changes that are of most importance to developmental practitioners we cannot reduce things of quality to quantities and little boxes. We end up considering only that part of what is important that is easily measured'. (Taylor 2003) Some go even further to suggest that 'if you can measure it, it isn't that important'. The reliance on numbers and counting creates a false precision about what is an inherently uncertain and evolving process. Yet taking a more qualitative approach is not an excuse for slackness. Taking a qualitative approach to assessing capacity building can be compared to a trial lawyer preparing a watertight case to prove 'beyond all reasonable doubt' that capacity building has made this or that difference.

To address the issue of assessing such complex processes, integrated, multi-dimensional frameworks are required. To this end, some practitioners are beginning to use more systemic or systems-based methods where the relationship between capacity and change can 'be framed as changes in the behaviour, relationships, activities or actions of people' (ECDPM, 2004). This approach explores the inter-relationship and influences between different elements and environments, both internal and external, and the different dimensions of organisational life (its internal functioning, programme of work, relationships and evolution).

While it is impossible to perfectly assess impact, clear good practice principles are emerging (Hailey et al. 2005), including.
- stakeholder involvement
- self-assessment
- triangulation
- balance of different methods and tools
- a simple system
- accept plausible association, not direct attribution
- recognise level of investment
- linking learning with action.

In addition, some simple, dynamic frameworks such as the Ripple Model (James 2002) are proving useful:

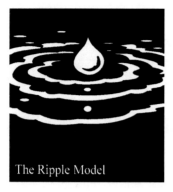

The Ripple Model

Using the analogy of capacity building being like a drop of rain which lands in water, we can see the impact as the ripples flow outwards at different levels. Initially there may be changes internal to the organisation in staff skills, systems, strategies and the like. These changes will ripple out in terms of bringing changes in relationship with other development actors, such as other CSOs or government. Ultimately we hope to see changes ripple out to the level of the beneficiaries of the client. The size and direction of the ripple is influenced by (and in turn influences) the context in which it moves.

Practitioners are also successfully experimenting with a number of innovative methods.

- The **Most Significant Change** methodology was used to review CABUNGO, a Malawian capacity building provider (Wrigley 2006). This methodology revealed changes in relations and power that other methodologies might have missed out. It encouraged the partner to take responsibility for their own learning from the evaluation by involving them partner in the analysis, and not just presentation, of the findings.

- **Participatory methods** such as ranking exercises, time-lines and scoring systems have been used. The ranking exercise and scoring exercises were able to elicit perceptions of the extent of change. These scoring systems are within an agreed organisational assessment framework and can be used and re-used over a period of time to give longitudinal information. A time-line enabled the impact of the capacity building to be weighed against other inputs to see whether positive improvements could be plausibly associated with capacity building interventions (James 2005).

- **Stories** as a means of measurement. CDRA (2001) argue that current development tools, such as donor-driven external evaluations based on logical frameworks, are very blunt instruments for measuring human change. Human change is too deep and complex to register with such superficial tools. Stories are a good way of 'sharing the richness and complexity of individual experiences' (Adams 2007:3). Stories can describe how relationships have changed over time. When we manage to express this then we will have something to say, something engaging, interesting and persuasive to put on the table in response to those who ask 'How do you know that your work has made a difference?'

It is clear that assessing the impact of capacity building is complex and onerous, but essential and possible. It will be more effective when it is connected to decision-making and takes place in an organisational culture where learning and experimentation is prioritised and embedded. The evidence suggests that successful impact assessment depends on a significant investment of funds (Hailey et al. 2005). It is therefore vital to provide the necessary time and resources. Impact assessment of capacity building should therefore be seen as an investment that can add value, rather than merely an additional cost.

Conclusion

Capacity building is not as confused as it initially appears. We know, in theory at least, quite a lot about what it is and how to do it well. We have clear good practice guidelines in terms of both the overall process and the methods/techniques. These guidelines are echoed by new thinking in management from other sectors. It seems we are on the right lines.

Not surprisingly, we see a consistency in these principles whether we are talking about individual development, community development, organisational development (business, NGO or government) social development or national development.

But the real question is whether we implement what we know. Do we practice what we are beginning to preach? Do we follow our own theory? Our rhetoric is only useful to the poor if we convert it into reality. We now take a need to take a hard look at how well we are doing in capacity building.

PART 3
Comparing Our Practice with Our Principles

art One shows that we have a coherent theory of capacity building. It is still evolving and not homogeneous, but in broad terms we know a lot about what capacity building is. Diverse stakeholders now agree that capacity building:

- is a complex, human process (which is therefore uncertain and unpredictable)
- is an internal process (endogenous)
- involves changes in relationship between elements of open-systems
- involves shifts in power and identity.

Part Two reveals we also know a lot about how to implement capacity building to maximise impact. We know that good practice capacity building:

1. is people-centred and engages with values
2. ensures client responsibility for change
3. addresses issues of power and relationship
4. involves a variety of techniques
5. explicitly adapts to the particular context and culture
6. uses and develops skilled local capacity building providers
7. pursues a carefully planned and 'situational' strategy
8. focuses on implementation of the change process
9. has developmental resourcing
10. systematically assesses and learns from experience.

In Part Three we examine uncomfortable, but important, questions. We ask ourselves, how well are we living up to our own standards in capacity building? Do we implement good practice in reality, or just write about capacity building in aspirational policy statements and funding proposals? Who holds us to account for implementing good practice? To move ahead, we need to have the self-assurance to face brutal facts and to admit we are not practicing what we preach.

We go on to explore the constraints that hold us back from doing what we know to be right. Resources and skills are insufficient but, the most important underlying problem is our attitude of self-interest.

CHAPTER 6

Heroines and Hypocrites: how well are INGOs performing?

In Chapters 3–5 we outlined our emerging theory of good practice in capacity building. We now know a lot about how it is meant to be done. In this section we find out how well international agencies are living up to our own benchmarks of a:

1. human and client-centred approach to capacity building
2. locally appropriate and sustainable delivery process
3. well-planned and managed process.

This chapter reveals that international agencies are often falling far short of their own standards of good practice. Performance is patchy. Two major studies in 2006 (Lipson and Warren 2006, World Bank 2006) highlight a number of areas where we are failing to practice what we preach. They echo the findings of an in-depth evaluation (in which one of the authors was involved) of an international NGO's decade of investment in capacity building. For reasons of confidentiality we shall call it 'TINGO', Typical International NGO.[5] These shortcomings in capacity building practice also resonate with other evaluations of capacity building performance that INTRAC has undertaken over the years (Sorgenfrei 2004; Beauclerk 2006 and 2007). Concerns about the efficacy of much capacity building work also marked much of the discussions at INTRAC's Capacity Building Conference 2006.

Obviously these findings are not true of all agencies everywhere, for some are better than others and within agencies the quality of programmes vary. But in general there is a large gap between our espoused principles and our actions which merits urgent attention. If we are serious, we need to have the courage to confront the brutal fact – that we are not adequately practicing what we preach. We need to ask ourselves hard questions and take a serious look at our practice to make capacity building work.

---

[5] Set up in the 1960s, TINGO operates largely through local NGO partners in about 50 countries. Its turnover is approaching $100 million a year, and it recently commissioned a major review of its capacity building strategy. Over the last ten years it has developed a reputation of being committed to, and promoting, innovative capacity building.

To what extent are we taking a human, client-centred approach to capacity building?

The evidence suggests that many capacity building programmes are not client-centred. They do not ensure that the client is taking responsibility for change. This is often because donors are tempted to impose their own analysis and try and control the content and process of the intervention too tightly. The majority of INGO respondents in INTRAC's survey did not allow local partners to fully manage any aspect of their capacity building work (Lipson and Warren 2006).

Client responsibility for change?

We know that capacity building is an internal process which has to address self-defined needs and purposes. But, in practice, many donors continue to impose their agenda for change. We inadvertently treat capacity building as if it were an exogenous process, something that we can successfully recommend, plan and deliver to others. Our capacity building practice contradicts what we know, because we have not engaged sufficiently with the crucial question of who sets the capacity building agenda.

The World Bank asserts the centrality of country ownership to any development processes, but discovered from its evaluation that 'in the area of public financial management... the countries do not fully "own" the change agenda' (2006:xv). We cannot merely reprimand the Bank for such a dichotomy between rhetoric and reality for it is also apparent in the way INGOs support capacity building.

Lipson and Warren's INGO survey illustrates how capacity building needs are still largely defined by Northern agencies (2006). The content of capacity building appears to reflect donor priorities, particularly in their changing context of 'results-based management' and 'risk assessment'. For example, over half of the major priorities for Southern capacity building clearly are aimed primarily at meeting Northern needs[6] for:

- project design and implementation
- monitoring and evaluation systems development and use
- impact assessment
- accountability
- financial transparency, systems and management.

The other three priorities: organisational development (OD) and change; strategy development and organisational learning may not necessarily be defined as needs by local NGOs.

These survey findings are reflected by the experiences of individual agencies like TINGO, which illustrate the strong European influence in setting the capacity building agenda:

---

[6] Obviously these may be beneficial to the Southern CSO, but are rarely prioritised by them unless they are thinking about what the donor wants to hear.

TINGO's Capacity Building Priorities

120 TINGO partners perceived that the main areas of capacity building that TINGO had supported were (in prioritised order):

1) Project Cycle Management (PCM)

2) Organisation Assessment and Development

3) Monitoring and evaluation

4) Strategy development

5) Proposal writing.

There was also a clear recent trend towards increased support for Governance, Financial Management and PCM. These closely correlate with TINGO's newly incorporated Risk Management system.

Survey results suggest that while INGOs emphasised CSO consultation and participation in shaping the capacity building work, only 37 per cent of the respondents (25 organisations) stated that they let local CSOs have total management of the capacity building (Lipson & Warren 2006:10). Thus, it appears that most INGOs prefer to retain control of the capacity building process themselves – designing the overall approach, making funding decisions and indeed directly delivering services themselves. This is well reflected in a confidential evaluation of a US NGO's capacity building programme in 2002 by one of the authors. In the words of its own staff:

- 'We give a lot of prescription'.
- 'We are desperate to have them adhere to our goals and consequently we have our feet on their necks'.
- 'We operate in an autocratic fashion. We believe that the main responsibility of subgrantees is to conform to our deadlines'.
- 'We dictate salaries and Conditions of Service. We prescribe what they should do'.

We could certainly do more to ensure that clients really take responsibility for change. As the example from Sri Lanka in Chapter 3 showed, the process for needs assessment can give very different responses depending on how the process is done and by whom. Passive acquiescence is not the same as active ownership. This illustrates the influence of power relationships in capacity building.

Power and Relationships?

While we understand that capacity building involves shifts in power and relationships (Beauclerk 2007, Wrigley 2006), the evidence from the evaluations also points to the relative low priority INGOs give to such issues. The 2006 INGO survey found that the subject of relationships with Northern partners/donors was second to bottom on the list of priorities. This may indicate that while INGOs accept the theory that capacity building involves shifts in relationship, they are more ambivalent in practice.

Only a minority of the INGOs expressed an understanding of capacity building as a two-way process of learning and change. The majority shied away from any reflections on the implications that a stronger local civil society might have for their own role in development.

To what extent are we supporting a variety of capacity building techniques though a local delivery process?

It is clear that INGOs support a wide variety of capacity building techniques, but training and technical assistance are still the most frequently used methods. INGOs support for local providers of capacity building appears to be more instrumental than strategic. They tend to contract them as one-off consultants, rather than supporting their staff and organisation development.

Methods?

According to the INGO surveys and evaluations, training and technical assistance are still the main methods of international agencies support for capacity building – despite the increasingly awareness of their limitations. The World Bank evaluation found that the "traditional tools – technical assistance and training – have often proven ineffective in helping to building sustained public sector capacity" (2006). The World Bank evaluation still concluded that the Bank's approach to capacity building was very training-oriented.

While many international NGOs use a variety of different methodologies, most continue to rely on training and technical assistance as the two most popular methods (Lipson and Warren 2006). As diagram below illustrates, nearly a third of those INGOs who responded to the 2006 survey placed a 'high' emphasis on these traditional capacity building approaches.

Yet it is clear from the many evaluations of different capacity building providers that a broader range of methods are actually practiced (Beauclerk 2006 and 2007). For example,

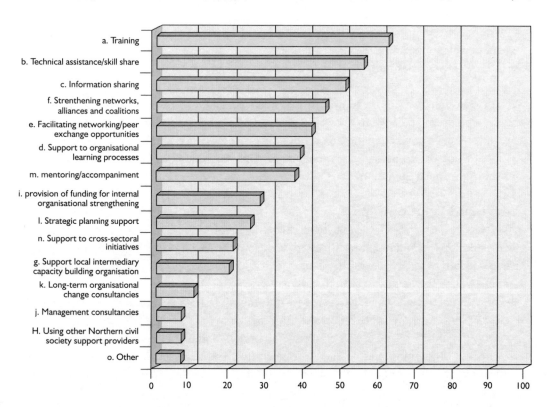

Sterland quotes capacity builders in the Balkans who report that 'longer-term mentoring, coaching, advice and facilitation is considered the only effective way to ensure the application of knowledge gained in training as well as to bring about change in individual and organisational attitudes.' (2006). INTRAC's capacity building work in Central Asia, which has been supported by ICCO, the Dutch Protestant NGO, incorporated such approaches as:

- organisational development
- accompaniment
- action learning sets
- modular training
- workshops & seminars
- conferences & roundtable discussions
- commissioning books and manuals
- action research.

Similarly, the evaluation of TINGO revealed it had used a diverse variety of models and methods. Interestingly training was still deemed the most effective capacity building methods from the survey of its 120 partners, but only when it is done well (in a modular format and with follow-up). These findings evaluation are outlined below:

TINGO Approach to Capacity Building

The partner survey revealed that partners perceived the five most effective capacity building methods as:

1. training
2. consultancy
3. publications
4. mentoring & coaching
5. staff advice

In all regions where TINGO operates training is still seen as an effective form of capacity building, particularly when it is in a modular workshop format, but only when systematically followed through. General workshops without follow-up have made little impact.

- Use of consultants was also very popular despite some concerns with their sustainability and cost-effectiveness.

- Publications are highly emphasised, illustrating the very high quality of TINGO's investment and performance.

- Mentoring and coaching is seen as the most effective capacity building method in Africa.

- Those who have been in partnership with TINGO for more than two years like exchanges and exposure visits as a useful way of learning.

TINGO international staff are concerned that they are supporting very expensive workshops with the wrong attendees present. Unless these events are systematically followed up they are worried that there is not much impact. All staff would like inputs to be more applied, tied to proper agreements, with outputs and timescales and interventions which move from training to on-the-job support.

Overall, training and technical assistance still appear the most commonly used approaches. This over-reliance on more structured approaches to capacity building suggests that many agencies are avoiding facing up to some of the messy and complex human dimensions of capacity building.

By inadvertently treating organisations as inanimate machines, rather than human systems, such organisations may be using the wrong tools. By relying on rigid planning frameworks we have reduced capacity building to a purely logical, mechanical process. The time-frames we use are based on a project cycle, not what pace of change is possible. Much of our capacity building work avoids (or merely pays lip-service to) sensitive or contentious areas such as cultural values and beliefs.

Spirituality, for example, is seen by many as impossible to address without getting into proselytising. Even many faith-based organisations are reticent about articulating what difference their faith makes to their work. And yet these values and beliefs are often what determine behaviour. Cross-cultural dimensions are also only rarely explored. It is often too sensitive to challenge deep-rooted attitudes of superiority or inferiority that often exist across cultures. Taking a technical approach to capacity building is much less threatening, easier to plan and more fundable.

Local Capacity Builders?

Twenty years ago the need for "the NGO community to develop its own OD and management services based in the South to provide local consultants, trainers, researchers and evaluators" (PAC 1986) was identified. Nearly half the respondents in the 1994 survey of INGO support to capacity building asserted that they provided support to Southern NGO training centres. Yet in the 13 years since then we have seen no real increase in INGO support to local capacity building providers. If anything, there seems to have been a shift from provision of core funding support to only hiring them on one-off contracts. The 2006 survey revealed that provision of direct support to local capacity building providers is now the least preferred approach (Lipson and Warren 2006). Only 20 per cent of the responding INGOs emphasised the importance of supporting them. Whilst nearly all saw providing partners with information about capacity building providers as part of the range of roles played, only three per cent (two organisations) indicated that they saw this as their primary role.

Capacity building may be becoming the new operational arena for international NGOs. In an effort to justify their role and income to their official government back-donors they are emphasising their own ability to build local capacity in the South. This in turn inhibits the development of local capacity building providers – a danger pointed out to INTRAC itself in its own work in Central Asia (Beauclerk 2007).

Part of the reason for this is that local capacity building providers are a scarce and possibly dwindling resource. Even existing capacity building providers are relatively fragile entities. One of the best known in Africa, Olive, has recently closed down – not for reasons of performance, lack of demand for its services or lack of income, but due to internal issues arising since the departure of its founder.

Other well-known African capacity building providers like CABUNGO in Malawi, CDRN in Uganda and TRACE in Tanzania may be vulnerable. Some are in a state of uneasy leadership transition and all face extreme challenges of financial sustainability. They face high staff turnover. Each of the four researchers involved in the INTRAC leadership study in 2003–4 has now left their capacity building organisation. Already two thirds of the researchers in the 2005 study on HIV and capacity building have also moved on. Many of these specialists have joined international donors like CIDA and Danida – who are supposedly supporting CSO capacity building. Local individuals who are trained and experienced in capacity building are a sought-after and mobile resource. Of the 15 local OD consultants that INTRAC has been involved in training in Malawi over the last ten years, only two are still with the capacity building organisation they were originally employed by (though five others are working as independent consultants). This situation is echoed in other parts of the world, including in Macedonia where financial constraints have forced MCIC to make four of their five capacity building staff redundant.

TINGO, however, provides a good example of an INGO taking the need to use and develop such local providers of capacity building seriously.

TINGO Support for Local Resource Pools

The lack of local capacity development providers sometimes means that the quality of capacity development services simply is not available, however much TINGO may want to follow principles of good practice. This is why TINGO has invested significantly in developing local resource provider pools. TINGO has been extremely innovative in training local consultants for capacity building work in Sudan, India and West Africa. They have also sought to contract out all of their HIV capacity building to a Uganda-based regional provider.

But overall there has been a lack of investment in development of capacity builders, and a failure to build a forum where they can share learning or develop good practice and a code of conduct. The need to prove quick results has prevented the strategic development of the sector. The well-meant intention to subject local capacity building providers to market demands for quality (by contracts for services rather than core funding), has inadvertently encouraged staff mobility. The best capacity building consultants are finding it financially more lucrative to work independently.

According to Alan Fowler, the formation of professionals in this field remains episodic and incoherent. While the odd donor may provide intermittent support, in general there is a lack of investment in promoting the quality and quantity of credible and experienced capacity builders (Fowler, 2006:7). This is reflected in lack of investment in the professional development of capacity builders; inadequate production of appropriate knowledge and resources and absence of time, places, means and systems for capacity builders to meet and exchange experience either within countries or across borders.

How well are we planning and managing the capacity building process?

The evaluations indicate that INGO support to capacity building is still ad hoc and disconnected.[7] There is limited oversight or integration of activities into a cohesive or strategic whole. We often fail to provide developmental funding to resource the implementation of change and we rarely undertake systematic monitoring and evaluation of our capacity building work.

A Strategic Approach?

Recent studies and evaluations of international agencies in capacity building reveal that they are strategic in name, but more makeshift in practice. A strategic approach involves being clear about realistic capacity building goals and ensuring that you adjust your systems to reinforce rather than undermine chosen goals. Again, the World Bank evaluation points out serious flaws in this area, noting that 'the Bank's support for capacity building in Africa remains less effective than it could be'. (2006:viii). A flavour of the findings are highlighted below (pp viii-xiv):

Evaluation of World Bank Capacity Building Support

- The international development community, including the World Bank, has traditionally treated public sector CB as a collateral objective – that is as a by-product or instrumental measure to advance near-term project outcomes – rather than as a core goal in its own right.
- The ability to implement CB activities is often over-estimated.
- Most projects do not specify CB objectives.
- CB activities are not founded on adequate needs assessments and do not include appropriate sequencing of measures.
- Most capacity support remains fragmented.
- The Bank has not yet established a knowledge base and guidance for its CB work comparable to those supporting its other main interventions.

Some two thirds of the INGOs who responded to the 2006 survey stated that they had a 'specific programme which is solely dedicated to civil society capacity building' (Lipson and Warren 2006). Yet despite this, the evidence points to INGOs not taking a coherent approach in practice. INGOs lack shared definitions of capacity building. They admit to 'scattered reference in diverse documents and policy papers' (ibid.). Fifty five of the 67 INGOs who responded to the survey did not have a formal policy framework for their work in this field – far less than in the 1998 survey.

The absence of a strategic approach leads to lack of consistency and coherence in the capacity building work undertaken across the organisation. Learning opportunities may be

---

[7] This is part of the justification for INTRAC's forthcoming Praxis Series volume 3 *A Framework for Capacity Building (a practical guide)*.

reduced, as there are no common conceptual, definitional and methodological references. Indeed, some INGOs responding to the 2006 survey mentioned that they found completing the survey a useful exercise, as it provided them with the opportunity to address issues that may not have otherwise arisen (Lipson and Warren 2006).

The evaluation of TINGO's work in capacity development revealed strikingly similar findings:

TINGO's Lack of Strategic Support for Capacity Building

Support to capacity building has been *ad hoc*, characterised by a succession of interesting one-off experiments, but no guiding or coherent strategy. As staff have joined or left TINGO the emphases in capacity building have shifted. Sometimes the capacity building strategy appears to have shifted as a response to new funding or partner fraud with consequent risk management concerns. There is much interesting information on TINGO's approach to capacity building in both published and internal documents, but these appear more individually-owned than organisationally-decided.

TINGO's approach to capacity building has been extensive, but scattered and inconsistent. It has too many focus themes that change regularly. This leaves partners overwhelmed by different priorities. TINGO's capacity building pushes for too fast a pace of change and is too short-termist.

Although capacity building is prioritised in the strategic plan, there appears to be more ambivalence in reality. The staff involved in capacity building have not had much power in the organisation to integrate it with the rest of TINGO's practice. The capacity building staff operate as an internal advisory service to the regional programmes, not an implementing department on its own.

Although capacity building is a strategic objective, it only merits one of 19 corporate indicators to measure TINGO performance (and there are grave concerns about the usefulness of that single indicator). Staff perceive that TINGO is largely driven by its grant management ('bank') function, not its capacity building objective. Most internal systems reinforce this priority and the sheer weight of work that grant management entails.

Shared understanding of capacity building is necessary both within each organisation, and also between the different stakeholders. There is little evidence of stakeholders taking sufficient time to reach joint definitions of terms before initiating a capacity building programme. Amidst pressure to sign contracts and reach deadlines, it appears easier to leave the definition and the different interests imprecise. Consensus is achieved by not clearly identifying the goal. This can often lead to inadvertent and passive acceptance of the agenda of many donors – to better demonstrate results and efficient grant management.

Implementation of change?

The performance of INGOs in supporting the implementation of change is mixed. There are examples of INGOs like ICCO in Central Asia or CORDAID in Malawi investing in follow-though. In other cases there is evidence that donors are more interested in supporting needs analysis and capacity building planning events rather than resourcing the implementation of change. It is often only the planning of the job that gets funded. Capacity building events, such as strategic planning sessions, HIV policy development processes and training courses, are what get funded. The better ones end up with action plans. But then the capacity building funding stops. There is often nothing planned or provided for the change process itself – such as HIV policy implementation (James 2006). All too often a donor funds a local CSO to develop an HIV policy, but then refuses to support its implementation. In addition, the capacity building provider (consultant/trainer) may move onto another client as 'the job is done'. But the real work of change, which only takes place back in the organisation, has not yet begun. As one respondent in a review of US NGO's support for capacity building lamented: 'we did not get support from the INGO in implementing the action plan'.

The lack of focus in capacity building programmes hinders the implementation of change. For example, one INGO in Africa identified between 20 and 50 capacity-building needs for each of its sub-grantees. As a result the local organisations were overwhelmed by the number of trainings and workshops and did not have the time to implement changes in their organisations. As one local CSO leader put it: 'What I have learnt I have locked up because I have not had time to implement'. Some were so involved with responding to the demands of the INGO for grant management requirements, the capacity-building work-shops, M&E and regular networking meetings that they felt they had effectively become employee of the INGO. Another NGO leader in Malawi estimated that he spent 50% of his time looking after INGO visitors – more as a tour guide than a leader of an organisation.

Developmental resourcing?

Clearly there has been significant investment in capacity building over the past 15 years. As we saw in Chapter 2, $15 billion a year is spent ostensibly on capacity building (DAC 2006). Forty five per cent of international NGOs responding to the 2006 survey estimated that they spend almost one-third of their overall programme funds on capacity building.

But there are growing concerns about quality and widening awareness that good prac-tice capacity building requires generous, but considered and careful support. Sida admits that the agency 'has not devoted enough attention to issues relating to the long-term financing of contributions to capacity development' (2000:25).

The quality of funding for capacity building is often compromised by donor funding systems that do not fit a more developmental approach. A recent review of Sida's work in this area pointed out the anomaly that while good practice principles of flexibility and ownership are highlighted in policy documents, grant management systems require very rigid specified results before starting (Bergstrom 2005).

Monitoring and learning?

The 1994 review of INGOs and capacity building concluded that 'evaluations of capacity building programmes by NGOs are extremely limited and there is little evidence from the NGOs regarding the effectiveness of their approaches...This is a significant problem given the ...' pressure from donors for evidence of impact' (James 1994). There has been some improvement since that time. A number of one-off evaluations of capacity building have and are taking place. Other INGOs such as SNV from Holland or SongES from Belgium, have invested in developing a very comprehensive system for measuring change resulting from capacity building. INGOs are now more able to provide examples and references of what they consider to be the impact of the capacity building work they are engaged in (Lipson and Warren 2006). However much of the commentary was qualified by statements on the methodological difficulties of measuring impact in this area of work. The review of INTRAC capacity building consultancies (Sorgenfrei 2004) highlighted that learning and impact assessment of capacity building is still weak.

It appears that, for the most part, we do not know whether capacity building programmes are really having intended impacts. This is not to say there has not been any impact, but we simply do not know. There is increasing experience of using innovative methods for monitoring and evaluation of capacity building, but we are not rigorous or disciplined in applying them. We remain ignorant of the best and the worst we do. TINGO's experience is typical of that of many agencies:

TINGO Evaluation Information

TINGO has not been obviously learning as an organisation from the wealth of capacity building initiatives supported. It does not know about the impact that its capacity building support has had. Some of the very remarkable and inspiring changes that have occurred in partners and communities as a direct result of TINGO support for capacity building are not known at the head office. This makes it impossible to celebrate success or learn from failure.

For this review it was surprisingly difficult to extract information about impact. Of the 57 projects identified by TINGO UK staff as representative of 'good practice' only two or three of the files (5%) contained anything approaching impact evaluation of the change. Many were just description of capacity building activities undertaken or planned and whether the capacity building grant had been spent accountably. The filing, in paper systems/archiving and on the computerised database, are difficult to use and do not facilitate knowledge management.

Conclusion

This chapter has highlighted some of the important differences between the principles we espouse in capacity building and INGO practice. It has not been an exhaustive evaluation of global practice, but has drawn on surveys of INGOs and individual agency evaluations. It has concentrated on where INGOs are falling short – not because there are no instances of good quality capacity building work, but because shortcomings point out areas for improvement.

The evaluation work that has been done in this area may not be comprehensive, but it does draw attention to significant weaknesses in those agencies that have had the rigour to look at their own practice in capacity building. Those that have not bothered to examine their practice are likely to be worse-off.

Only by facing the facts of our failures can we change and make capacity building work. But in order to improve, we must first go deeper and identify the forces that constrain us.

CHAPTER 7

Contradictions and Constraints: Why do we not implement good practice?

'We are not responsible for changing the world, but we are responsible for changing what we can within our sphere of influence'.
Brian Pratt INTRAC Conference 2006

'The number one constraint is self-interest. It is holding us back and we do not talk about it'.
Brenda Lipson INTRAC Conference 2006

This book has so far shown that we know how to do capacity building well, but we fail to implement it in practice. The obvious next question is to ask why do we not follow what we know about good practice? This chapter recognises that the answer will be different for every organisation but that there are four overarching constraints: the global aid context; donor and international INGO funding; capacity building providers and CSO clients.

The image below illustrates this relationship in a simple way:

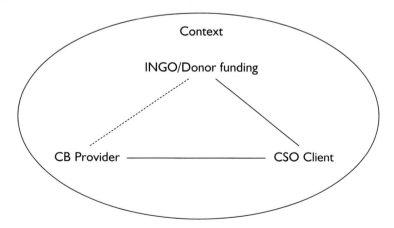

Whichever stakeholder group we belong to, some of these constraints are outside our influence and control. It is easy to see ourselves as helpless victims of bigger forces – the aid system, our donors, or our management. But we know that some of these factors are within our sphere of control and influence: we can advocate with those further up the aid system to take policy decisions that make our capacity building context more enabling and change the way we work.

We need to identify and work on the constraining forces. We will see in this chapter that these constraints exist in our strategies, skill, systems and resources. Ultimately, however, the underlying factor is a lack of commitment to overcome our inherent self-interest. Our attitudes are the root causes of our failures.

Constricting Context

We saw in Chapter 2 how recent global trends are affecting capacity building. These inhibit our ability to implement the good practice that we know. We saw how civil society capacity building takes place in a harsh environment – marked by volatile political and economic circumstances; growing numbers of vulnerable people living in abject poverty; on-going devastation and distress caused by conflicts and disasters; an HIV pandemic decimating and distracting human development capacity and emigration of skilled workers to Europe and North America. Such a context throws up extreme and, to a degree, intractable capacity building challenges. In such an adverse environment, even just capacity maintenance may be a remarkable, if unacknowledged, achievement.

Furthermore, the capacity gap, between those organisations that have knowledge, expertise and the web and those who do not, is growing. The proliferation of knowledge has lead to a widening space between North and South, rich and poor, and those with access to the capacities that deliver such knowledge. These capacities maybe as simple as having education or funds for a training budget, but must also now include access to the Internet and other technologies. Knowledge capacity is more than information. It is also about networking, developing new contacts, getting hold of resources and becoming confident in 'development speak'. Increasingly civil society is divided not just by the size of an agency or its special interests, political affiliations or ideological agendas, but also by access to new information technology.

We also saw in Chapter 2, discernible shifts in the aid context. Funds previously available for civil society are now being channelled through government. Most donors (though not all), are opting to take a 'harmonised' approach to funding as enunciated in the Paris Declaration of March 2005 (see information box in chapter 2). In practice, civil society is relegated into a contracted-out social welfare provision role.

Economists are now emphasising the primacy of economic growth as they did in the 1960s and 1970s. There has been a related privatisation of aid, both in terms of shifting focus towards supporting the private sector, as well as contracting out aid projects. The audit-orientation of public sector management has permeated the aid world. Donors are increasingly driven by measures of efficiency – disbursing large sums of money in a simple, cheap way and in as short a time as possible. There is often a trade-off between the quality and the quantity of aid given.

Many elements of the aid system act as major disincentives and, in some cases, prevent implementation of good quality capacity building. For example, the increasing preoccupation with proving quantifiable results within a short, project-based period makes it harder to take a long-term approach. The need for the aid system to disburse large sums of money quickly prevents an incremental approach to capacity building. The need for CSOs to be able to absorb significant sums of money can push CSOs way beyond their competence too quickly. Competitive bidding processes require organisations to prove they already have adequate capacity and give them no room to identify or admit weaknesses and plan how to address them. The underlying theory of the aid system is that we can influence significantly, if not control, another country's development. We just have to push in the right places, finance, incentivise, penalise and measure the right things.

Such trends influence the activities of both international NGOs and local CSOs. We see international NGOs becoming more operational, moving away from 'partnerships' with local organisations to 'strategic alliances' on the basis of sub-contracts. In many places, local CSOs are struggling to survive.

Donor and international NGOs

But everything cannot be blamed on the constricting aid context. Just as some businesses are able to thrive in declining industries, so capacity building can work in a harsh environment. The reasons for our failure to implement what we know are deeper than simply the context. Donors, both official agencies and INGOs, do not always follow good capacity building practice because they:
* lack understanding and knowledge about capacity building, particularly at senior level
* are driven by resources, not mission
* make decisions on the basis of fear and self-interest.

Lack of senior management knowledge

Although we now know a lot more about capacity building this knowledge does not always permeate throughout the whole organisation. Capacity building specialists and evaluators may be moving to some form of common agreement about concepts and approaches but, this does not necessarily mean that those who make the decisions are on board. Capacity building specialists tend not to have formal power in INGOs – they are often in the innovative, but marginal, part of the structure. TINGO's experience illustrates this well:

> **The powerlessness of capacity builders within TINGO**
>
> 'The staff involved in capacity building have not had much power in the organisation to integrate capacity building with the rest of TINGO's practice. There has been no director of capacity building. The small team is set up as an internal advisory service to the regional programmes, not an implementing department on its own. Currently most institutional memory of capacity building exists in one relatively junior staff.'

Those who do not work directly in capacity building tend to under-estimate the degree of difficulty and thus push for overly ambitious targets. In other sectors, such as small enterprise, it is recognised that only about 20 per cent of small businesses survive their first five years. But all 100 per cent CSOs on the receiving end of capacity building are expected, not just to survive, but to become stronger. This is probably unrealistic.

Driven by resources, not mission

International agencies are intermediaries, raising money from donors and spending it on grants and activities. They are inherently pulled in two different directions. Good practice capacity building may say one thing, but good practice fund-raising may say the opposite. Which voice shouts loudest? Who gets listened to? Today capacity building practice tends to suffer when pitted against fundraising opportunities. It is a courageous INGO manager who turns down future funding on the grounds that it does not fit easily with good practice capacity building.

In the scramble to increase or maintain turnover in an increasingly competitive market, international NGOs and donors are adjusting policies and procedures to fit with the new aid architecture. To secure large contracts and grants, international agencies are tempted to simplify capacity building into over-ambitious plans. There is rarely time for consultation with local CSOs, let alone to allow them to 'take responsibility' for the capacity building. Donors are under pressure to deliver quick and unrealistic results.

Once funding is secured, the accountability obligations can foster a consolidation of international control. Compliance becomes the name of the game. INGOs are pushed into 'micro-managing' partners to deliver according to pre-set targets. All this of course flies in the face of good practice capacity building (and all other forms of human and social development). For example, using local capacity building providers appears as expensive and outside the control of international donors. This is why there is still a tendency to take a 'do-it-yourself' approach to capacity building.

Information systems are set up to serve the needs of those controlling the money. Donors develop accountability-oriented systems, not capacity building-oriented systems. For example, Bergstrom notes that 'Sida's internal rules are not in harmony with this view of the importance of process orientation (in capacity building)' (2005). When there is a conflict between the two, accountability is often prioritised above impact.

Self-interested, 'fearful' attitude

The preoccupation with funding is symptomatic of a deeper question of attitude. The Northern-orientation of Southern capacity building needs we saw in Chapter 6 illustrates this. Despite the rhetoric, capacity building needs are frequently defined as what affects the donor – project proposal writing, reporting, financial management and monitoring and evaluation. Capacity building for CSOs is what will help the donor disburse funds, provide accountability and manage risk. Capacity building is too often undertaken primarily for a donor purpose.

Furthermore, the international NGO refrain of 'trying to work ourselves out of a job' has not been heard for some time. Self-interest has come to the fore. In some contexts we see INGOs becoming more operational, displacing local CSOs and taking the place of local capacity building providers. They are undoubtedly distorting the market for local CSO staff:

Where has all the capacity gone?

From my experience in Malawi working with both international and local NGOs over the past ten years, I estimate that there are more than three times as many Malawians working for international NGOs as there are working for local NGOs.

Assuming there are 20 INGOs with an average of 200 staff = 4,000 INGO staff
Assuming there are 300 local NGOs with average of 4 staff = 1,200.

And we wonder where the local CSO capacity is!

Source: Rick James (author)

Fears undermine international agencies' commitment to operationalising good practice capacity building. It is easier to talk about shifts in power and relationships in principle, than to apply them to actual relationships with local CSOs. In other cases, it may be fear of failure – apprehension of what may be found – that holds INGOs back from more systematic monitoring and evaluation of capacity building. There is a concern that all the investment in capacity building has not brought about the changes that were hoped for. So it may be better not to know.

Some of these constraints in attitude reflect basic aspects of human nature. We do not practice what we know in capacity building because we all succumb to 'deadly sins'.

Constraining attitudes in Capacity Building

Pride – seeing ourselves as better than others (hubris).
Pride is behind the thinking we have encountered amongst all stakeholders: 'we know better what others need'; 'we are OK, but they have a problem'; 'we can control how others develop'; 'we do not need help from others'; 'I cannot admit my faults'; 'we do not need to work with others'.

Greed – the acquisition of wealth or a longing to possess something.
Preoccupation with securing more funding or fees has undermined the practice of many stakeholders, pushed international agencies to take over work that could be done by local CSOs and prioritised accountability to donors over impact on the poor.

Envy – a desire to have something possessed by another.
Envy may be at the root of our failure to collaborate with other stakeholders in capacity building. Local capacity building providers see others as competition and fail to work together and learn from each other. International agencies pull local CSOs in different directions with 'their' capacity building activities.

Apathy – reluctance to work or make an effort and failure to use/develop talents.
Different stakeholders sometimes do not bother to apply their knowledge and are too lazy to prioritise. We do not actively seek to develop and implement our knowledge about capacity building. We often fail to have the determination to see it through.

Limited Capacity Building Providers

The shortage of credible and experienced capacity building providers is an undoubted constraint on implementing good quality capacity building.

Lack of Local Knowledge and Skills
The skill set required for providing high quality capacity building services is very demanding. In Chapter 4 we saw that good quality providers:
- recognise and respond sensitively to the influences of culture and context
- develop client-ownership of the process to focus on their motive for change
- take a people-centred approach to change, work with the personal and manage tensions creatively
- see and work with the inter-relationships between elements
- sensitively and courageously understand and challenge power dynamics
- have the competence to use a variety of methods, including the more experiential
- balance structure and flexibility
- communicate in a culturally sensitive and creative way.

There are not enough individuals who are able to meet such demanding criteria to implement good practice capacity building. This general skill set also changes as the context introduces new challenges. For example, in much of sub-Saharan Africa, it is now vital for African CSOs to mitigate the impacts of HIV/AIDS on their workforce. To remain effective in a changing context, capacity building practitioners may need to add to their skills the ability to help CSOs take a proactive response to HIV/AIDS.

Capacity building providers are also sometimes guilty of letting their competencies skew the process. Like the proverbial carpenter with a hammer, who sees every problem as a nail, so capacity building providers can see their competence as the solution to every problem. So monitoring and evaluation trainers see that CSOs needs M&E training while OD providers see the need as OD processes. Given that every CSO has capacity needs in almost every area, there is ample temptation for capacity building providers to prioritise their own areas of competence (albeit inadvertently).

There is a felt need for greater professionalism in capacity building but also concerns about how to obtain it. There are not many fora for capacity building providers to learn from each other. CDRA in South Africa convenes a bi-annual OD Event and INTRAC runs periodic conferences as well as working with local providers to build capacity and encourage linkages with other providers. Impact Alliance has developed a community of capacity building practice. But compared with the overall need, such fora are a drop in the ocean.

Sustainability of Human Resources
The supply of local capacity building providers has undoubtedly grown in the last 15 years. New organisations started in different parts of Africa, particularly during the 1990's: such as TRACE and EASUN in Tanzania; CABUNGO and CADECO in Malawi; Olive and CDRA in South Africa and CDRN in Uganda. Similarly capacity building providers have emerged in

Eastern Europe (such as MCIC; Civic Initiatives); the Middle East (such as Zenid, PNGO); China and Central Asia (NPO Network, CIB).

However, since the late 1990s this growth suddenly stopped. The number of capacity building institutions is contracting, particularly in Eastern Europe and Africa. Some have closed down, such as Olive in South Africa while others have downsized and lost staff. All are facing considerable challenges. They meet a vital need, but are in a fragile state, starved of human, leadership and financial resources. There are a variety of reasons for this.

Initially capacity building providers face the challenge of establishing credibility and even a market for their services, particularly in newly emerging civil society sectors. Once they have got over that hurdle, local capacity building providers find it difficult to keep well-trained staff, particularly in places where the demand for capacity building skills far outweighs the supply (driving fees up). Individuals would prefer to see consultancy fees coming into their own pockets. They are tempted to become independent consultants. We also saw in the last chapter, how instead of developing local capacity building providers, donors are in fact draining them of some of their best staff by offering them distorted remuneration packages.

The sustainability of local capacity building providers is also challenged by questions of leadership (as with most CSOs). Many of the organisations that have emerged over the past few years are still led by the founder. There are very few examples (other than CDRA) of capacity building organisations that have successfully moved on following the departure of their founder and even fewer documented.

Financial Sustainability

One of the major challenges facing local capacity building providers is securing sustainable financial resources. Alan Fowler observes an increasing financing difficulty for those capacity building suppliers whose practice is not applied to a particular area or sector of development – health care, HIV/AIDS, microfinance, environment or conflict prevention (2006).

Donors, understandably emphasise the benefit of local providers operating as a business and charging consultancy fees for services. They have moved away from providing core grants to such organisations, let alone providing any endowment funding. The high fees that providers thus charge have a number of implications:

- encouraging the staff mobility described above
- skewing the client-base towards larger local CSOs, international agencies and the private sector: some donors are also encouraging local capacity building providers to spend their limited time working outside the CSO sector
- discouraging providers from spending time reflecting and learning from their experiences
- discouraging providers from providing un-contracted follow up: to make ends meet local capacity building providers have to quickly move onto the next job
- encouraging providers to accept contracts for work that do not embody good practice principles.

Attitudes

While many capacity building providers do an excellent job in difficult circumstances, some providers are not as good as they might be. This may not just be a question of resources or skills, but one of attitude. They sometimes:

- do not have the courage and determination to see through difficult, time-consuming processes
- respond to the donor as the real client, rather than the CSO
- do not have the commitment to relentless improvement or to gender equality
- compromise on principles and values in order to get contracts (i.e. by providing a kick-back to whoever is offering the contract)
- concentrate on the weaknesses of clients in order to portray themselves as 'experts'.

Activity, survival-oriented client CSOs

Southern and Eastern CSOs are not always innocent victims in the failure to practice good quality capacity building. To some extent, and in some circumstances, they also constrain good practice. For some, their pre-occupation with action and short-term financial survival prevents them from looking honestly and internally at their own organisations. They are caught in a relentless spiral of activity, too busy to stop and think about their own future capacity needs and to plan accordingly.

The frequent preoccupation with short-term survival has blinded many CSOs to their own capacity issues. When asked what is needed for them to improve, the knee-jerk response is 'more money!' In some cases, their main concern becomes how to pay salaries at the end of the month, rather than what difference they are making in the lives of poor people. The focus has shifted from impact to survival. So the capacity building is merely viewed as a means to an end – of getting grant funding. This is often a problem of poor vision and leadership within CSOs. One respondent in a capacity building evaluation commented that while 'strategic planning is important, there is the underlying assumption that leadership is inspiring and committed and relationships are OK. If there are problems at this level then there will not be much change'.

International agencies tend to blame partners for problems and vice versa. Rather than recognise their own weaknesses in order to address them, many CSOs feel more comfortable blaming others. They have limited ownership of capacity building, not because the opportunity for taking ownership is not there, but because they have become comfortable in the victim role. This may be related to a lack of self-worth and dignity, pride in refusing outside help or a fear of change.

In analysing the challenges of becoming a learning organisation, Adams points to the challenge of 'breaking through the constraints of being 'too busy to learn' and having the discipline demanded to sustain such processes' (2007:3). He also asserts that it requires courage and humility and: 'an openness and willingness to admit your own ignorance and knowledge gaps'. (ibid:12)

Such challenges are also illustrated by the fact that few CSOs in sub-Saharan Africa identify responding to HIV and AIDS within their organisation as a capacity building need. Many CSOs are in denial about the impact of the pandemic on their work lest it affect their standing with donors (James 2005). Research with NGOs in Uganda, Tanzania and Malawi indicated a number of internal organisational issues that constrained their capacity to respond to HIV and AIDS. Avoidance of HIV and AIDS-related issues may be symptomatic of reluctance to address constraints hindering gender mainstreaming within CSOs or taking a rights-based approach.

CSO Internal Constraints on HIV/AIDS Capacity Building

Putting Values into Practice: Some respondents asserted that CSOs are not responding to HIV because they do not act according to their stated values. As one CSO leader bluntly admitted: 'Many of us are briefcase NGOs existing only for self interest'. Such CSOs are not really concerned about looking after the workforce.

Unsupportive Leadership: Some leaders lack knowledge about HIV or the skills to deal with infected staff. Some CSO leaders' lifestyles are perceived as 'reckless' and these leaders may not push their organisation to respond to HIV, because they fear if they do, they will be exposed themselves.

Organisational culture: The organisation's culture may promote denial (particularly within FBOs). Effective and appropriate responses are blocked when stigma exists in the organisation's culture, if it is gender-insensitive or has a hierarchical power culture.

Short-term strategy: Many CSOs are failing to analyse the external environment, instead basing responses to HIV on whether individual staff members fall sick. CSOs' focus is also on making a difference 'out there' in the lives of communities and not spending time on themselves. It is also exacerbated by pride: 'We think we are better off than those we are teaching'.

Weak finance and human resource systems: Many CSOs lack knowledge of the actual costs of HIV/AIDS as weak systems of human resource management, finance and monitoring and evaluation constrain their ability to respond, or even to budget and allocate funds to do so.

Lack of staff competence: Respondents cited the lack of skills or confidence in the ability of human resource departments to deal with HIV/AIDS.

Lack of financial resources: Budgets are funded by donors and tied to projects. CSOs still perceive most donors as unwilling to support the internal costs of responding to HIV (seen as driving up overheads). Donors were perceived to be interested in 'trimming CSO budgets'.

Taken from James, 2006

Conclusion

This section has examined how well we are living up to our own standards in capacity building. Do we implement good practice in reality, or just write about capacity building in aspirational policy statements and funding proposals?

A number of factors that constrain our ability to implement good practice capacity building have been identified. We need to address each of these constraints if we are to consistently build good quality capacity. The factors in the global aid environment have been identified. The preoccupation with short-term measurable results – with development viewed as a safety net for security purposes – undoubtedly raises questions for official donors: why invest in long term CSO capacity building. But it is easy to blame the context and blame others for our failures in capacity building.

There is a lack of knowledge and skills in capacity building amongst all stakeholders. Underfunding of capacity building clearly also undermines impact. The way in which resources are given to capacity building is not set in stone but can be changed,.

Ultimately, however, many of these factors arise from each stakeholder allowing self-interest to drive their engagement in capacity building – but not having the courage to admit it.

The root cause of our failure to implement good practice capacity building is that we succumb to self-interest, or a victim/dependence mentality. Our self-interest dilutes our commitment to capacity building. We do not implement what we know because in our hearts we are ambivalent. We must recognise the contradictions between our espoused values and our actual practice and choose to change. We need to heed the words of Monica Sharma of UNDP who has noted that 'in the context of global development, analysis clearly reveals that the underlying causes of under-development and the patterns that perpetuate it – the deep-rooted, almost hidden ones – lie in the domain of personal and social attitudes, perceptions, beliefs, practices and norms. These then, should be the areas of principle concern.' (2006:21)

The ways forward require us to address our underlying attitudes. Instead of succumbing to our vices, we should develop our virtues. We need the self-assurance to face brutal facts about ourselves and commitment to practice what we preach.

PART 4
Ways Forward

We have seen that:

1. Capacity building is an internal process: outsiders can only cultivate or create favourable conditions and give appropriate inputs, but cannot control.

2. Capacity building is a profoundly human process of change: it is complex, relational and political and must deal with individual self-interests and fears, not just amorphous institutions.

3. 'Universal' good practice principles of capacity building exist, but these need to be applied differently in different situations.

4. We are not doing well enough in putting what we know into practice.

5. Lack of resources and skills inhibit implementation, but it is our contradictory attitudes and self-interests that ultimately constrain us.

In Part Four we go on to highlight the importance of working on our own underlying attitudes. We need the humility, honesty, determination and courage to collaborate with others to implement the good practice that we already know.

CHAPTER 8

Taking Responsibility
for Moving Forward

*'Never doubt that a small group of committed citizens can change the world.
Indeed it's the only thing that ever has'.*
Margaret Mead, quoted by Senge et al 2004: 138

'Development is all about coming together to take responsibility for changing a situation'.
Brian Pratt, INTRAC Capacity Building Conference 2006

We saw in the previous section that our implementation of good practice in capacity build-ing is patchy. There are pockets of good practice, but overall considerable gaps still exist. We are not consistently practicing what we preach. In part this is due to constraints of skill and resources. More fundamentally it is our own attitudes and self-interest that holds us back.

If we do not change, the future of capacity building is bleak. There will be some progress, where enlightened stakeholders practice what we know to work. But for the most part, if hidden self-interest predominates and none of us take real responsibility for our own change, then nothing fundamental will shift. Things will be worse in 20 years time, not better.

Yet because capacity building is a human process, change is possible. Impassioned leaders can inspire positive change. Committed groups can turn things round. The poten-tial is there. Sufficient resources exist. We know what to do. There are good examples to learn from.

Implementing good quality capacity building is undoubtedly difficult, but not impossi-ble. If we have the will, the determination and commitment we can overcome contextual, resource and skill constraints.

Chapter 8 identifies potential ways forward. We initially look at addressing constraints: the contextual constraints at a policy level; the resource constraints for donors; and the skill constraints of capacity building providers. Ultimately, however, we need to address deeper, heart-felt attitudes. To really make capacity building work we have to deal with the under-lying self-interested attitudes that constrain our impact. It may not be very technical. The virtues we need to make a difference may appear to some as too 'touchy-feely' and simply not economic enough. But unless we cultivate and develop these virtues, all our beautiful

capacity building plans and programmes will be in vain. We need:
1. humility to change ourselves and collaborate with others
2. honesty and openness about our own self-interests
3. a sense of social justice to put the interests of the poor above our own
4. discipline to take capacity building seriously
5. courage and faith to let go of control and trust people to develop themselves.

These virtues only exist in action, not theory. We therefore go on to outline a number of practical actions we can take to improve our capacity building practice – virtuous capacity building for the future.

Actions to address contextual constraints

The context has a profound impact on how capacity building can be implemented. All stakeholders can contribute to making the context for CSO capacity building more favourable. There are a number of ways to do this and these will differ between stakeholders and in different contexts. The 2006 INTRAC Capacity Building Conference suggested a few practical steps forward.[8]

Addressing contextual constraints

We can advocate with those at a 'higher' level to take policy decisions that create a more favourable environment for capacity building. This might involve:

- continuing the dialogue on the effects of the Paris Declaration on civic space/CSOs and CS strengthening
- work to influence the 2008 Accra meeting and ensure that the topic is included via debates/workshops at key events leading up to it
- donors building understanding of civil society within their own governments and creating enabling legislative frameworks
- establishing small groups to develop an understanding of civic-driven development
- making efforts to expand the constituency for civil society and build awareness and support
- urging donors to clarify policy on civil society and capacity building and make explicit and coherent statements.

Actions to address lack of knowledge and skills

We have also seen that capacity building is constrained by a lack of shared knowledge and skills. There are instances of decision-makers not having the knowledge to implement good practice. Leadership decisions are taken on the basis of what is good for funding, rather than what is good for capacity building. Furthermore we have seen that there are not always

---

[8] See www.intrac.org/pages/CBprogramme.html for full report

enough capacity building practitioners with the skills to facilitate change effectively.

There are a number of ways we can improve the skill limitations of INGOs and capacity building providers. We can also take policy decisions to avoid international 'poaching' of local capacity. This may involve choosing to work more with local partners rather than implementing international programmes or making changes in recruitment policies. It may entail advocating with others to stem the haemorrhage of local talent from many of the neediest parts of the word.

There are other ways we can bring together the learning in this field and to ensure its wider dissemination. The INTRAC Conference participants highlighted some concrete commitments in this area:

Addressing lack of knowledge and skills

- having a 'clearing house' to collect, synthesise and disseminate existing knowledge on capacity building topics, events, workshops, conferences and learning initiatives on diverse topics
- building a base of impact information: one group/organisation could collect and analyse stories and initiatives of capacity building successes
- increasing the opportunities and improving the methods for shared practitioner learning through an annual forum; topic-based learning groups; flexible, horizontal and plural exchanges and ensuring resources for learning time are an integral part of funding capacity building initiatives
- developing our own competencies and knowledge, in particular with regard to the 'soft' areas such as building respect/trust and emotional intelligence in relation to inter-organisational relations
- supporting others to develop their capacity building.

Actions to address lack of resources

There are a number of creative ways to address the lack of resources both financial and organisational in capacity building.

We can make considered investments in strengthening local capacity building providers. We can prioritise the development of local capacity building practitioners, both as individuals and as institutions. There is a need for more formation programmes that increase the supply of local capacity building providers in many parts of the world. This is a costly and somewhat indirect investment, but without it capacity building will be constrained.

Subsidising the consultancy fees charged by local CSOs would avoid the lure of seeking international clients which can leave them too busy for local clients. This would also reduce some of the imperfections in the labour market, whereby it is financially lucrative for trained local facilitators to leave their capacity building institution and set up as independent consultants. Such funding could provide local organisations with time and space to think, reflect and learn from experience.

Addressing the lack of financial resources in capacity building may not be simple, but it is certainly possible. The participants at the 2006 INTRAC Conference made specific suggestions on how to address the lack of resources to support good capacity building work

---

Addressing lack of resources

- establishing a broad civil society-controlled Trust Fund for Civil Society Capacity Building with a pool of money from different sources
- increasing investment in local support provision
- increasing opportunities for local providers to offer services
- exploring ways to professionalise provision: there is currently little or no formal structured formation of capacity building providers and hardly any university courses on this specialism.

Actions that address our values and attitudes

We saw clearly in the previous chapter that the character we bring to capacity building is one of the most important determinants in making it work. Our attitude is more important than the skills or the resources we have at our disposal. We know from experience that individuals and groups have inspired change on the basis of their underlying attitudes. Both PRIA in India and CDRA in South Africa are good examples of capacity building institutions that have made just such a difference.

- In mid-2007, PRIA, possibly the foremost Southern capacity building institution, celebrated its 25th birthday. It has made a considerable contribution to changing the face of capacity building. Its director, Rajesh Tandon, was the leading light behind the creation of the Southern-led International Forum on Capacity Building.

- CDRA's resolute attention to a 'developmental process' has shaped capacity building practices of providers throughout Africa. More remarkably, they have increasingly influenced the practice of donors, particularly in Holland, Sweden, Germany and Belgium.

But we do not need to wait for others to inspire us, before capacity builders can take responsibility themselves. The 2006 INTRAC Conference identified a number of ways in which capacity builders can start holding themselves to account and assist others to do the same.

Addressing attitudes

- developing codes of practice and statements of principles for capacity building
- implementing self-regulation based on accountability for practising our values
- developing peer accountability or 'critical friends'
- encouraging capacity building providers to form/join 'Communities of Practice' (groups of people actively involved and exchanging learning in an issue)
- developing processes which enable the users of capacity building services to hold service providers, facilitators and donors to account
- building on existing and developing new methods for assessing impact.

Virtue-based Capacity Building

Ultimately we all need to cultivate and practice five life-giving virtues to counteract our tendencies to slip into constraining attitudes. We need

1. humility to change ourselves and collaborate with others
2. honesty and openness about our own self-interest
3. a sense of justice: willingness to put the interests of the poor above our own desire for growth
4. discipline and determination to take capacity building seriously
5. courage and faith to let go of control and trust people to develop themselves.

We need to be clear about these ideals, but also know that such virtues are never fully realised for they are subject to ambiguities of power and priorities. We have to acknowledge that no situation is completely free from self-interest. It is not a question of compromising our values but of holding onto them tightly. Even in messy and complicated situations we can use them as benchmarks in decision-making about capacity building.

We need **humility** to take responsibility, first and foremost, for our own change. We must explore how we have contributed to the capacity building challenges of today and ask what we have to change in ourselves in order to enable others to change. We need to be able to confront the brutal facts about ourselves – to see where we have been hypocritical. We are good at pointing out the problems in others, but less inclined to hold ourselves to account.

We need the humility to recognise that we cannot do it ourselves. Are we ready to invest the time, care, diplomacy and commitment in working with others to solve issues? How ready are we to relinquish control? Are we open to our own learning and help from others? Collaboration and consensus amongst stakeholders is essential to achieve development 'ends', even if it makes the 'means' more vulnerable and complicated. If we do not actively collaborate with other NGOs we cannot advocate for donors to work together. If we cannot collaborate effectively within civil society we will not be able to advocate with integrity for others to do it. In any capacity building process we need the humility to want to understand and work with different, and not always complementary, agendas and interests and to negotiate an agreed purpose.

We also need the **honesty** to be aware and open about our self-interests. These will not disappear when they are brought into view, but it will make them more manageable. When our interests clearly conflict with the ultimate goal of capacity building, we have to subjugate them to the better good.

We need our sense of **justice** to remain passionate about the goal of development. How easily we get diverted into more self-centred goals of growth. It is all too easy to lose sight of the end, in our efforts to increase the means.

We need to be **disciplined** about our work in capacity building, determined to put good theory into practice. Reflective spaces for learning do not arise by accident. We need disciplined thought and actions, realistic goals, clear strategy, good practice methods, rigorous monitoring and evaluation systems, innovative organisational learning, flexibility and accessible documenting. We need to acknowledge that we cannot manufacture capacity. As Dawit Zawde said at the INTRAC conference: "we get achievements the old-fashioned way – through sheer hard work". We need the determination to see it through, for change takes time. It took Wilberforce 44 years from the time he first challenged Parliament in 1763 to overseeing the abolition of slavery in 1807. This would not go down well today in an age which demands quick immediate results and numerical proof of impact

Finally we also need the confidence and **faith** in ourselves and others that change is possible. It takes courage to let go of control and trust people to develop themselves. But we also know that this is the only way development will take place.

CHAPTER 9

Capacity Building:
A Concluding Overview

In this book we have been primarily concerned with the challenges of capacity building in civil society, and in particular building the organisational capacities of CSOs. The conclusions are relevant for capacity building at other levels too: individual, community, sectoral and societal. Organisational capacity building can be seen as conscious and holistic interventions designed to improve an organisation's effectiveness and sustainability in relation to its mission and context.

We hope that this review of the literature and practice around capacity building has helped demystify some of the conceptual confusion, highlighted aspects of good practice and identified some of the challenges faced by capacity builders. Our review of the literature and our experience suggests that capacity building is an elastic concept ill-suited to precise definitions. But there is a consensus among stakeholders that it:

- is a complex, human process
- is an internal process
- involves changes in relationship between elements of open-systems
- involves shifts in power and identity
- is uncertain and unpredictable
- can refer to building capacity at a societal, organisational or a personal level.

For those working in the area of aid and development, capacity building works at many different levels – from building the capacity of local community-based organisations to developing public services or promoting good governance.

The lack of a tight framework for analysis has allowed a multiplicity of meanings and interpretations to emerge. As a consequence, we need to clarify our own understanding of the term to avoid misunderstandings. This is also important because the target or focus of capacity building initiatives is varied and diverse.

There is a broad spectrum of capacity building targets. These vary from helping a specific individual to develop him/herself, to facilitating community and organisational change, to promoting wider social changes at a regional or national level. Whichever end of the spectrum the work is focused at, one conclusion stands out – capacity building is about change to the lives of individuals and communities. Well-designed and well-implemented capacity building interventions can result in significant change to how organisations work and how managers manage. They can help promote innovation, ensure greater sustainability, help redefine relationships and increase levels of participation and community involvement. Such interventions encourage new ways of working that will benefit the poor and most marginalised.

Capacity Building: Good Practice

The evidence suggests that donors and NGOs alike see capacity building work as a priority. With the increasing number of people living in abject poverty, coping with humanitarian disasters and the repercussions of global warming or pandemics like HIV-AIDS there is growing understanding of the need to develop local institutions and infrastructure. As a result there is increasing recognition of the importance of investing in the organisational and management capacity of CSOs. This makes more effective use of scarce resources and helps develop their role in shaping policy and mobilising local communities. The need for civil society capacity building is not just restricted to poverty alleviation, for there is also increasing awareness of the need for civil society strengthening in higher income countries. The adverse impact of lack of social capital is to be found across the globe.

We have argued throughout the book that successful capacity building should be client- and people-centred, promoting local ownership and empowering individuals or groups of people. It should energise communities and organisations. Thus capacity building is about releasing latent human ability and promoting mutual learning and trust. But capacity building is also a political process. It is about engaging with, and where appropriate changing, centres of power (both formal and informal). The political nature of capacity building should not be underestimated and capacity builders need to factor in how best to handle the dynamics of power in their work.

Our analysis identifies capacity building as a complex human process whose success is determine by its ability to adapt to local cultural and contextual conditions. It is an endogenous process that involves changes in power and relationships, and the outcome of which is neither certain or predictable. Effective capacity building is a holistic process which works at many levels. It is not just about engaging with individuals at an intellectual or technical level, but also at an emotional and even spiritual level. It is a dynamic process focused on changes to attitudes and relationship.

Good practice in capacity building therefore has to incorporate the personal and the cultural. It is about 'unleashing' particular talents or behaviours but also about promoting and facilitating change and renewal – overcoming anxieties and developing confidence. In essence, it is about encouraging learning and embedding new learning in organisational values and ways of working. While learning and change are closely related – some would say learning is synonymous with change – it is clear that such capacity building processes also depend on the quality of leadership available. Good leadership in capacity building is not just promoting a vision. It is as much about steering the process of capacity building through its many iterations, and helping all involved to grow, develop and cope with the consequences of the change process in which they are engaged.

Capacity builders have an array of tools and techniques they can use to facilitate such processes. These range from changing personal attitudes and competencies through training, shadowing, attachments or coaching to wider organisation development processes that shape institutional cultures and structures. They need be applied in a timely and sensitive manner using local expertise, and adapted to different cultural dimensions. But the evidence also suggests that good capacity building relies on a degree of forethought and planning.

Capacity building is an inherently complex process involving many different individuals and stakeholders. Timing is crucial, as is the ability to apply different styles, techniques and methodologies at different stages in the process. Appropriate incentives need be factored in and sufficient resources budgeted for. All those affected by any capacity building process need to have real and valued incentives to encourage their involvement in the process. Such incentives can be tangible (e.g. financial or involving promotion) or intangible (e.g. improved morale and better team dynamics), but need to be provided in a timely and appropriate manner.

While plans, budgets and schedules need to be devised that are appropriate to the type of organisation, they also should adapt and evolve as the process progresses. All the evidence suggests that during the course of any capacity building intervention improvements and changes in one area have a way of placing unexpected new demands elsewhere. Consequently, attention to measures with ongoing monitoring is essential, not just to assess progress, but also to assess the unforeseen consequences of interventions. Plans are therefore at best indicative, and good capacity builders rely on ongoing monitoring to judge how processes need to evolve.

Thus, it is clear that we need to learn from experience and use impact assessment methodologies to gauge the effectiveness and value of any particular capacity building initiative. The debate should not be about the choice of method used, but how they are applied. It is essential to make the process as important as the product – to create simple, participative methods that use different processes to examine the dynamic and multi-dimensional character of what they are trying to measure.

We know that there is concern about the cost of capacity building and whether such programmes are really cost-effective and deliver what they purport to. Some of these issues can be addressed through greater stakeholder participation, using a mix of methods and tools and better analysis and dissemination of findings. While these may be time consuming and expensive, they are a worthwhile investment if the ultimate purpose of impact assessment – to identify long-term and sustainable change – is to be achieved. Efforts to assess the contribution of capacity building should be seen as a long-term investment that both assesses impact but also contributes to performance improvement and new learning. This, in turn, highlights the importance of 'intelligent accountability' and the need to analyse and disseminate findings in an engaging and timely manner.

Capacity building: future trends

In many ways capacity building in civil society is about investing in, and accumulating, social capital. It is not just about developing the capacity of separate institutions. In future the focus of much capacity building work may shift to promoting more dynamic collaborative work within civil society itself. Capacity builders may become increasingly engaged in facilitating the development of new networks, strategic alliances, consortia and mergers between NGOs. Linked to this will be ongoing work to ensure the credibility and reputation of the sector through greater accountability and the establishment of effective governance mechanisms. This will include development of management boards and establishment of new ethical practices or codes of conduct. There will also be increased emphasis on the crucial role of individuals in leadership roles or as social entrepreneurs. Consequently we expect to see more of capacity builders' time invested in mentoring and coaching, as well as performance management tools such as 360-degree appraisals.

Capacity building will also need to adjust to the changing social context. We have seen that globalisation and urbanisation are already having an impact on capacity building. Providers of such services will need to adjust their work to answer the difficult question of how to create and maintain civil society capacity in increasingly mobile societies?

As to the process of capacity building, we can expect to see much more innovative use of interactive web-based tools in promoting change, delivering training and personal coaching and generally sharing experiences. Capacity building is an important element of the knowledge economy. In our increasingly networked society it is imperative that capacity builders should use such media to close the knowledge gap and facilitate transformational interventions. Capacity builders themselves may benefit from building specialist fora or networks for capacity builders where they can share experience, exchange ideas, explore innovative approaches and develop their profile and craft in a safe and neutral space.

But the real challenge is how we actually do our work and how we implement and fund effective, appropriate and sustainable capacity building. We need to invest in the development of a new generation of capacity builders to help implementation, and establish new mechanisms to fund the investment needed. This is partly about identifying and ring-fencing funds for ongoing capacity building work and employing specialist capacity builders. But it is also about developing new types of capacity building trust funds, social enterprise investment trusts or venture philanthropy initiatives (whereby capacity building funds are repaid at low interest rate or in kind once an organisation is well-established with its own sustainable income stream). Capacity building is an investment for the future and should be judged accordingly.

Capacity building: making it work

While much of the book has explored the characteristics of effective capacity building we are still left with the difficult issue of why, despite all our knowledge and experience, capacity building interventions commonly fail to meet expectations. There are a number of influences and constraints at work today that undermine our ability to implement appropriate and effective capacity building interventions. These include the impact of the aid new orthodoxies, the institutional imperatives of donors, the lack of skills and understanding in many CSOs as to how to implement effective capacity building and the limited number of credible and experienced capacity builders willing and able to work with CSOs.

In conclusion it is apparent that we know what to do, but that our efforts are not always successful. There are a number of explanations for this including the reality that the capacity building process is often not owned by the organisations themselves but still dominated or determined by powerful external stakeholders such as the donors or partner INGOs. They are able to impose their own agendas or planning technologies such as programmatic planning or log frame analysis. There is also concern that powerful partners, whether they be donors or INGOs, are able to enforce their own analysis of what needs to be done. This is all too often characterised by a dependence on training-based solutions and other forms of direct technical assistance, rather than holistic long-term organisation development processes or cultural change initiatives.

It is a matter of some concern that while donors are willing to fund specific events (such as a strategic planning exercise or a series of training workshops) they appear less willing to stump up the money for ongoing implementation of a change process. There seems to be an over-emphasis on the planning or competency building elements of many capacity building initiatives, rather than implementing the changes required. As has been emphasised previously, this state of affairs is aggravated by the impact of current aid orthodoxies, uncertainty as to the role of civil society organisations and an over-emphasis on accounting for resources rather than ensuring the overall mission is achieved.

Part of the problem also lies with the CSO community itself and the failure of their staff to grasp the complexity and challenges of implementing capacity-building processes successfully. This is partly because of unwillingness to effect major changes that threaten the status quo and jeopardise individual positions or roles. It is partly because of an understandable unwillingness to invest considerable time and resources in a process that deflects attention from programme work or detracts from direct contact with beneficiaries. And also partly because of a lack of expertise in implementing capacity building work, and little understanding of the complexities inherent in such organisational change initiatives.

This situation is not helped by the shortage of reliable, experienced local consultants who can advise and facilitate the capacity building process. The credibility, experience and expertise of those facilitating are crucial. A skilled capacity builder does not simply apply different approaches or techniques, but also knows how to gain the trust and respect of the parties involved and is able, above all, to handle different agendas and the power dynamics involved.

Successful capacity builders working with CSOs are still relatively rare. The evidence suggests that those with sufficient skills are attracted to work elsewhere, and that there are no obvious institutions to promote the work of such capacity builders or develop their competencies. It is also noteworthy that while a number of specialist organisations, such as INTRAC in the UK, PRIA in India and CDRA in South Africa were established in the late 1980s, few new specialist capacity building institutions have been established in the last ten years.

Does this reflect a lack of engagement in developing the capacity of civil society organisations, or complacency about the availability of suitable skills and competencies?

One can but conclude that effective capacity building depends on the skill and insight of the capacity builder, and her/his ability to work with different groups and cope with the expectations of the different stakeholders. Such individuals and teams need the ability to understand the context and culture in which they work and to appreciate the dynamics of the relationships between the key players. There has been a lack of investment in development of capacity builders, and a failure to build a forum where they can share learning, develop good practice or a code of conduct. The need to prove quick results has prevented the strategic development of the sector.

The availability of skilled and respected individuals to champion any capacity building initiative or change process is major determinant of failure or success. As such, capacity building depends on the skill and commitment of the people involved. It may appear that capacity building is primarily concerned with developing institutions and infrastructure, but in reality it is a human process that depends on the active engagement of many different individuals, teams and communities.

Underlying attitudes are at the heart of what we do well and also what we do badly. To build capacity more effectively requires that we address resource, skill and knowledge constraints. But ultimately it also requires grappling at a deeper, more human, level. We need to become more aware of how our own self-interests, our greed and our pride are the major enemies of capacity building. We have to become more aware of them in order to consciously contain them. To address the complexities and challenges of capacity building, we need to cultivate and tightly hold onto life-giving virtues. The foundation of effective capacity building in a rapidly changing world is to practice age-old virtues of humility, honesty, justice, determination and hope.

Bibliography

Adams, J, (2007) Learning and Accountability: A Monitoring and Evaluation Consultant's Perspective, *Praxis Note 32*, INTRAC, Oxford. Downloadable from http://intrac.org/pages/PraxisNote32.html

Adair, J. (2002) *Effective Strategic Leadership*, McMillan, London.

Anheier, H.K. (2005) *Non Profit Organisation: Theory, Management, Policy*, Routledge, London.

Ashman, D. (2001) *Building Alliances with Civil Society*, IFCB.

Ashman, D. (2005) *Supporting Civil Society Networks in Institutional Development Programmes*, AED Center for Civil Society and Governance, Washington DC.

Barney, J., (2006) *Gaining and Sustaining Competitive Advantage*, 3rd Edition, Prentice Hall, London.

Beauclerk, J. (2006) *Evaluation of Ecumenical Consortium for Central Asia*, Internal INTRAC report

Beauclerk, J. (2007) *Strengthening the Capacity of Strategic NGOs in Macedonia*, Internal INTRAC report, Oxford.

Bergstrom, L. (2005), Development of Institutions is Created from the Inside, Sida Studies in Evaluation 05/04, Stockholm.

Black, L. (2003) Critical Review of Capacity Building Literature and Discourse in *Development in Practice*, Vol. 13, No. 1, Feb pp 116–119

Bradley, B., P.Jansen, & L.Silverman, (2003) 'The Non Profit Sector's $100 Billion Opportunity', *Harvard Business Review*, Vol.81(5), pp.94-104

Brehm, V.M. et al (2004) *Autonomy or Dependency: Case Studies of North-South Partnerships*, INTRAC, Oxford.

Britton, B. (2005) *Organisational Learning in NGOs: Creating the Motive, Means and Opportunity*, Praxis Paper No.3, Oxford. Downloadable from http://intrac.org/pages/PraxisPaper3.html

CDRA (2001) *Measuring Development: Holding Infinity*, Cape Town.

Collins, J. and Porras, J. (1997), *Built to Last: Successful Habits of Visionary Companies*, Harper Business, New York.

Cooke, B, & Kothari, U. (eds.) (2001) *Participation: The New Tyranny*, Zed, London

Cracknell, B. (2000), *Evaluating Development Aid: Issues, Problems and Solutions*, Sage, London.

Crooks, B. (2004) *Working without Words: Exploring the Use of Cartooning and Illustration in Organisational Capacity Building* Praxis Note 7 Downloadable from http://intrac.org/pages/PraxisPaper7.html

DAC Network on Governance (2006) *The Challenge of Capacity Development: Working towards good practice*, Downloaded Oct 2006 www.worldbank.org/INTCDRC/Resources/oecd_challenge_of_capacity_development.pdf

Datta, D. (2007) *Appreciative Approach to Capacity Building: The Impact of Practice*, Praxis Note 28, INTRAC, Oxford. Downloadable from http://intrac.org/pages/PraxisNote28.html

Deans, F, Oakley, L., James, R. and Wrigley, R. (2006) *Coaching and Mentoring for Leadership Development in Civil Society*, Praxis Paper 14, INTRAC, Oxford. Downloadable from http://intrac.org/pages/PraxisPaper 14.html

Eade, D. (ed.) (2000) *Development and Management*, Oxfam, Oxford.

Eade, D., (1997) *Capacity Building: An Approach to People-Centered Development*, Oxfam, Oxford.

Ebrahim, A. (2003) *NGOs and Organisational Change*, Cambridge University Press, Cambridge.

Edwards, M. & Fowler, A. (eds.) (2002) *Reader on NGO Management*, Earthscan, London.

European Centre for Development Policy & Management. (2003) 'Evaluating Capacity Development', *ECDPM Newsletter*.

Eyben, R. (ed.) (2006) *Relationships for Aid*, Earthscan, London.

Fowler, A. (2006), *Systemic Change for Promoting Local Capacity Development, Working Paper for SNV*, Johannesburg

Fowler, A. (2005) *Aid Architecture: Reflections on NGO Futures and the Emergence of Counter-Terrorism*, INTRAC OPS 45, Oxford.

Fukuda-Parr, S., Lopez, C. and Malik, K. (eds.) (2002) *Capacity for development – New Solutions to Old Problems*, UNDP, Earthscan.

Green, B. and Battcock (2003) 'Capacity Building: A buzz word or an aid to understanding?', *Developments*, DFID, London.

Gibelman.M & Geluna, S. (2001), 'Very Public Scandals: NGOs in Trouble', *Voluntas*, Vol.12.1

Goleman, D., Boyatzis, R. McKee (2003) *The New Leaders: Transforming the Art of Leadership into the Science of Results*, Time Warner, London

Hadjipateras, A. with Abwola S. and Akullu, H. (2006) *Addressing Stigma in Implementing HIV/AIDS Workplace Policy, an ACORD Experience in Uganda*, Praxis Note 21, INTRAC, Oxford.

Hailey, J. (1999) 'Ladybirds, Missionaries and NGOs: Voluntary Organisations and Co-Operatives in Fifty Years of Development', *Public Administration and Development*, Vol.9.5

Hailey, J. (2000) 'Indicators of identity: NGOs and the strategic imperative of assessing core values', *Development in Practice*, Vol.10.3

Hailey. J & Smillie, I. (2000) *Managing for Change: Leadership, Strategy & Management in South Asian NGOs*, Earthscan, London.

Hailey, J. (2000), 'NGO Partners: The Characteristics of Effective Development Partnerships', in S.P.Osborne (ed.), *Chapter in Public-Private Partnerships: Theory and Practice in International Perspective*, Routledge, London.

Hailey, J. & James, R. (2002), 'Learning Leaders: The Key to Learning Organisations', *Development in Practice*, Vol.12. 3 & 4

Hailey, J. (2004), 'Trees Die from the Top: International Perspectives on NGO Leadership Development', with Rick James, *Voluntas*, Vol.15.4, pp.343-353

Hailey, J. & Sorgenfrei, M. (2004) *Measuring Success: Issues in Performance Measurement*, Occasional Paper 44, INTRAC, Oxford.

Hailey, J. (2005) *Rising to the Challenges: Assessing the Impacts of Organisational Capacity Building*, with Rick James and Rebecca Wrigley, Praxis Paper 2, INTRAC, Oxford. Downloadable from http://intrac.org/pages/PraxisPaper2.html

Hailey, J. (2006) NGO *Leadership Development*, Praxis Paper 10, INTRAC, Oxford. Downloadable from http://intrac.org/pages/PraxisPaper10.html

Handy, C. (1991) *Waiting for the Mountain to Move: and Other Reflections on Life*, Arrow, London.

Howard, S. (2002), 'A spiritual perspective on learning in the workplace', *Journal of Managerial Psychology*, Vol. 17 No. 3 pp 230–242, MCB University Press.

Hudson, M. (1999) *Managing Without Profit*, Penguin, London.

Hudson, M. (2003) *Managing at the Leading Edge: New Challenges in Managing Non-Profit Organisations*, Directory of Social Change, London.

James, R. (1994), *Strengthening the Capacity of Southern NGO Partners: a Survey of Current Northern NGO Approaches*, OPS 5, INTRAC: Oxford.

James, R., Ryder, P. & Elliott, S. (1998) *Survey of Northern NGO Approaches to Capacity-Building*, Unpublished Report compiled for the International Working Group on Capacity-Building (IWGCB), INTRAC: Oxford.

James, R. (ed.) (2001) *'Power and Partnership: Experiences of NGO Capacity-Building'* INTRAC, Oxford.

James, R. (2002) *People and Change*, INTRAC, Oxford.

James, R. (2002), 'Practical Guidelines for the Monitoring and Evaluation of Capacity Building' Occasional Paper 36, INTRAC, Oxford. Downloadable from http://intrac.org/docs/OPS36.pdf

James, R. (2003): Leaders Changing Inside-Out: What Causes Leaders to Change Behaviour? Cases from Malawian Civil Society. The International NGO Training and Research Centre INTRAC Occasional Papers Series No: 43 Downloadable from http://intrac.org/docs/OPS43final.pdf

James, R. (2004) *Creating Space for Grace*, Stockholm, Swedish Mission Council Downloadable from http://www.missioncouncil.se/download/18.5b4c3f30107c27e2cd580007929/04_2_space_for_grace.pdf

James, R. (2005a), *Building Organisational Resilience to HIV/AIDS: Implications for Capacity Building*, Praxis Paper No. 4, INTRAC, Oxford. Downloadable from http://intrac.org/pages/PraxisPaper4.html

James, R. (2005b) 'Quick and Dirty' Evaluation of Capacity Building: Using Participatory Exercises', *Praxis Note 15*, INTRAC, Oxford. Downloadable from http://intrac.org/pages/PraxisNote15.html

James, R. (2005c) 'Vision Quest', *Praxis Note 17*, INTRAC, Oxford. Downloadable from http://intrac.org/pages/PraxisNote17.html

James, R. (2006) *The Organisational Impacts of HIV/AIDS on CSOs in Africa: Regional Research Study Uganda, Malawi, Tanzania*, INTRAC Praxis Paper 13, Oxford. Downloadable from http://intrac.org/pages/PraxisPaper13.html

James, R. & Wrigley, R. (2007) *Investigating the Mystery of Capacity Building: Learning from the Praxis Programme*, Praxis Paper 18, INTRAC, Oxford. Downloadable from http://intrac.org/pages/PraxisPaper18.html

Kaplan, A., (2002) *Development Practitioners and Social Process: Artists of the Invisible*, Pluto Press, London.

Korac-Kakabadse, N., Kouzmin, A. and Kakabadse A. (2002), Spirituality and Leadership Praxis, *Journal of Managerial Psychology*, Vol. 17 No. 3 pp 165-182, MCB University Press.

Lebow, R., and Simon, W. (1997), Lasting Change, Wiley, New York.

Lewis, D. (2001) *Management of Non-Governmental Development Organisations: An Introduction*, Routledge, London.

Light, P. (2004) *Sustaining Non Profit Performance, The Case for Capacity Building*, Brookings Institute, Washington D.C

Lipson, B. & Warren, H. (2006), *International Non-Governmental Organisations' Approaches to Civil Society Capacity Building: Overview Survey*, INTRAC Paper for Capacity Building Conference, Oxford. Downloadable from http://intrac.org/pages/CBProgramme.html

Lusthuas, C., Adrienne, M-H. and Perstinger, M., 1999, *Capacity Development: Definitions, Issues and Implications for Monitoring and Evaluation*, UNDP/UNICEF.

Malunga, C. (2004), 'Using African Proverbs in Organisational Capacity Building', *Praxis Note 6*, INTRAC, Oxford. Downloadable from http://intrac.org/pages/PraxisNote6.html

Mboizi E. and James, R. (2005), 'Robbed of Dorothy: The Painful Realities of HIV/AIDS in an Organisation', *Praxis Note 12*, INTRAC, Oxford. Downloadable from http://intrac.org/pages/PraxisNote12.html

Missika-Wierzba,B and Nelson,M, (2006), 'A Revolution in Capacity Development? Africans ask Tough Questions', *Capacity Development Briefings*, World Bank Institute, No. 16

Moore, M. (1996) 'Promoting Good Government by Supporting Institutional Development' *IDS Bulletin*, Vol 26.

Morgan, P. (2006), *The Concept of Capacity*, ECDPM, Maastricht.

McKinsey and Company (2001), *Effective Quality Building in Non-Profit Organisations*, New York.

Partnership Africa Canada, (1986), *Partnership Matching Rhetoric to Reality*, Ottawa.

Pearson, J. (2006) *Organisational Learning Across Cultures*, INTRAC Praxis Note No. 20 Oxford. Downloadable from http://intrac.org/pages/PraxisNote20.html

Pratt, B. (2003) *Changing Expectations: The Concept and Practice of Civil Society in International Development*, INTRAC, Oxford.

Reality of Aid (2006) ActionAid, London.

Sahley, C. (1995) *Strengthening the Capacity of NGOs: Cases of Small Enterprise Development Agencies in Africa*, INTRAC, Oxford.

Sen, K. & Pratt, B. (2006) Capacity Building in the Context of New Aid Effectiveness Programmes, Unpublished draft of Capacity Building Conference Paper, INTRAC, Oxford.

Sen, K. (2007) 'The War on Terror and the Appropriation of Development', *ONTRAC 35*, INTRAC, Oxford.

Senge, P., Scharmer C., Jaworski J. and Flowers, B. (2004) *Presence: Human Purpose and the Field of the Future*, Society for Organizational Learning, Cambridge MA.

Sharma, M. (2006) 'Conscious Leadership at the Crossroads of Consciousness', in *Shift: at the Crossroads of Consciousness*, No 12.

Squire, C. (2006) *Building Organisational Capacity in Iranian Civil Society: Mapping the Progress of CSOs*, Praxis Paper 8, INTRAC, Oxford. Downloadable from http://intrac.org/pages/PraxisPaper8.html

Sorgenfrei, M. (2003) *Current Issues in Capacity Building Provision*, Internal INTRAC report, Oxford.

Sorgenfrei, M. (2004) *Capacity Building from a French Perspective*, Praxis Paper 1 INTRAC, Oxford. Downloadable from http://intrac.org/pages/PraxisPaper1.html

Sorgenfrei, M. and Buxton, C. (2006) *Analytical Skills Training in Central Asia*. Praxis Note 22 INTRAC, Oxford. Downloadable from http://intrac.org/pages/PraxisNote22.html

Sterland, W. (2006) Civil Society Capacity Building in Post-Conflict Societies: The Experience of Bosnia & Herzegovina and Kosovo, Praxis Paper 9, INTRAC, Oxford. Downloadable from http://intrac.org/pages/PraxisPaper9.html

Symes, C. (2006) Mentoring Leaders of HIV/AIDS CBOs, Praxis Note 24, INTRAC, Oxford. Downloadable from http://intrac.org/pages/PraxisNote24.html

SNV in a Nutshell, 2007–2015 Strategy Document

Taylor, J. (2003), *Using Measurement Developmentally*, CDRA, Cape Town.

Tebeje, A. (2005), Brain Drain and Capacity Building in Africa, downloaded from internet 28.11.2006. www.idrc.ca/en/ev-71249-201-1-DO-TOPIC.html

UNDP (2005) Human Development Report, http://hdr.undp.org/reports/global/2005/ downloaded 21/2/07

UNDP, (2006) Capacity Development Practice Note, downloaded from internet 27.11.06 www.capacity.undp.org/index.cfm?module=Library&page=Document&DocumentID=5599

Wagner-Marsh, F. and Conley, J. (1999) 'The Fourth Wave: The Spiritually-Based Firm', *Journal of Organizational Change Management*, Vol. 12 No. 4 pp 292-301, MCB University Press.

Whyte, A. (2004) Landscape Analysis of Donor Trends in International Development, Human and Institutional Capacity Building Series No.2, Rockefeller Foundation, New York.

World Bank (2006) Capacity Building in Africa: An OED Evaluation of World Bank Support, http://www.worldbank.org/oed/africa_capacity_building/

Wrigley, R. and Prince S (2007) Organisational Learning in Civil Society: Influences of Culture, *Relational Dynamics and Informality* Praxis Paper 17, INTRAC, Oxford. Downloadable from http://intrac.org/pages/PraxisPaper17.html

Wrigley, R. (2006) *Learning from Capacity Building Practice – Adapting the 'Most Significant Change' (MSC) Approach to Evaluate Capacity Building Provision by CABUNGO in Malawi*, Praxis Paper 12, INTRAC, Oxford. Downloadable from http://intrac.org/pages/PraxisPaper12.html